Freedom
Beyond
COMPREHENSION

Freedom *Beyond* COMPREHENSION

Joan HUNTER

WHITAKER
HOUSE

FREEDOM BEYOND COMPREHENSION:
Severing Your Painful Past

Joan Hunter Ministries
P.O. Box 777
Pinehurst, TX 77362-0777

ISBN: 978-1-60374-505-5 ✦ eBook ISBN: 978-1-60374-522-2
Printed in the United States of America
© 2012 by Joan Hunter

Whitaker House
1030 Hunt Valley Circle
New Kensington, PA 15068
www.whitakerhouse.com

Library of Congress Cataloging-in-Publication Data

Hunter, Joan, 1953–
  Freedom beyond comprehension / by Joan Hunter.
    p. cm.
  ISBN 978-1-60374-505-5 (trade pbk. : alk. paper) 1. Spiritual healing—Christianity. 2. Healing—Religious aspects—Christianity. I. Title.
  BT732.5.H795 2012
  234'.131—dc23

                2012019149

3 4 5 6 7 8 9 10 11 12 ᙡ 20 19 18 17 16 15 14

Contents

Foreword 9

Introduction: No Strings Attached................................ 11

   1. The Toll of Trauma... 13

   2. Stress Has Serious Consequences 35

   3. Wired but Tired... 45

   4. Erase the Pain of Your Past................................. 59

   5. Walking in Deliverance 85

   6. Don't Look Back.. 95

   7. Discover Your True Identity................................ 103

   8. Drawing Closer to God 119

   9. A Love Beyond Comprehension 131

About the Author.. 139

Foreword

If you have met Joan Hunter in person, you know exactly what we mean when we describe such a meeting as an "unforgettable experience." The joy, energy, and charisma that surround this woman are contagious and liberating! As we have learned more about her painful past and the obstacles she has overcome, we have come to realize that she has the authority and wisdom that are gained only by walking out the principles of God and standing firmly on faith in Jesus Christ.

The journey to uncovering buried pain can seem like an uninvited interruption. But it is a crucial step if one is to laugh easily and love life again. In *Freedom Beyond Comprehension*, Joan draws from both real-life stories and her vast knowledge to help us learn to embrace God's complete healing for our past wounds while disarming the lodged memories that hold us captive. This book is an excellent and engaging resource for individuals, parents, and ministers who truly desire to live out their true heritage as children of God and enjoy the limitless blessings that are rightfully theirs.

Our marriage was tested by the crisis of an affair, complete with the pain of betrayal and complicated by an unexpected pregnancy. Psychologists told us that even if our marriage survived, we would never trust one another or enjoy complete safety in our relationship ever again. Today, we want to shout with joy from the housetops: "Our Redeemer lives!" Our God has the supernatural power to take our ashes—our buried pains, our deep regrets, our anguish and grief—and exchange them for beauty.

We wrote this on October 7, 2012—the eleventh birthday of our son Robert. Not only did we decide to keep the baby, but my husband gave him his very own name, so that Robert would never have to wonder for even one day of his life whose son he is. He is not an accident, a mistake, or the result of a sexual affair; he is a gift that was entrusted to our family, just as our other three children were.

In the same way, *you* are a gift. The Lord had a dream of you before He created you. And He put you on this earth at exactly the right time. You may have experienced pains that your Father in heaven never intended for you to bear, but, through Jesus and the power of the Holy Spirit, He wants to heal you completely. Jesus wants you to be *free*—free from the fear that it will happen again, and free from any sense of rejection or loss. You don't have to remain in the prison of the past for even one more day. As you read *Freedom Beyond Comprehension*, let the anointing of God's presence saturate you with peace as you receive the most powerful gift of all: unconditional, perfect, and extravagant love.

—*Audrey and Bob Meisner*
Best-selling authors, *Marriage Undercover*, and TV hosts, *My New Day*

No Strings Attached

Trauma. It affects all of us, at one point or another. Sometimes, it affects us physically, leaving behind visible scars and tangible brokenness. Other times, it comes in the form of an emotional ordeal or a mental blow that devastates our hearts, infiltrates our minds, and imbeds itself in our memories. Whatever its form, trauma is a powerful experience, and its effects are far more pervasive than most people probably realize.

As a minister who travels extensively throughout the world, I have met people who have suffered every kind of trauma imaginable. *Imaginable* is really a misnomer, though, because some people's stories are so despicable, the imagination struggles to conceive anyone even surviving such experiences. The trauma is incomprehensible—literally beyond comprehension.

In such extreme cases, what hope is there for healing and restoration? None, if the victims rely on human methods alone. But when the divine is introduced—when God comes on the scene—healing isn't just a possibility. It's a promise. *"With God all things are possible"* (Matthew 19:26; see also Mark 10:27). God is all-powerful, and He alone has the ability to erase the pain of past experiences and release us to walk in freedom, enjoying the *"life in all its fullness"* (John 10:10) that Jesus came to give us.

Yet many believers, even those who have turned their traumas and pains over to the Lord, struggle to live in this freedom. The reason is a failure to release the past. We have a part to play in the process of getting free. We must let go completely, severing every tie that binds us to the people, events, and experiences that have caused us harm. The truth is, Jesus can take our pain only as far away as we let Him.

In this book, we will discover how to do just that: how to release the pain of our pasts completely to Jesus, no strings attached, and march forth in true freedom—a *Freedom Beyond Comprehension*.

CHAPTER 1

The Toll of Trauma

Trauma is one of the most common causes of illness. It has incredible power to open the doors of our bodies to sickness. When you experience something traumatic, it's kind of like an emotional earthquake in your body. It causes everything to "shift," and not in a good way. The 9.0-magnitude earthquake that shook Japan in 2011 actually caused the earth's axis to shift.[1] And that's what happens in our bodies and minds where trauma is concerned. Trauma gets our bodies out of alignment. It disturbs the electrical, chemical, and magnetic frequencies of the human system. And then, before we know it, stress comes on the scene and produces stress hormones, which inhibit the function of the immune system. That's why we hear so many prayer requests for autoimmune diseases.

It's important for you to fortify your immune system and its functions, because you're exposed to sickness wherever you go. Shopping at the mall, traveling by plane, and even sitting at home, you come across a myriad of germs and bacteria. And there is only so much you can do to protect yourself. So, it's important to keep your immune system strong. But it won't be strong as long as you're suffering the aftermath of trauma. In this chapter, we're going to explore how to be healed of trauma and its far-reaching effects.

IT ISN'T "JUST IN YOUR HEAD"

Trauma manifests in multiple forms. Just do a Google search of the term "trauma" or "cellular memory" to learn about the physical effects

---

[1] http://content.usatoday.com/communities/sciencefair/post/2011/03/japan-earthquake-shifted-earth-axis-shorter-day-nasa/1.

of trauma, even trauma that was not physical in nature. After someone goes through a traumatic experience, ill effects manifest usually within six months to a year. And it is documented that when trauma comes in, it affects every cell in your body and will remain inside your cells until you die—unless God takes it away.

It is legitimate to make a connection between emotional trauma and physical symptoms. Take, for example, the medical condition *takotsubo cardiomyopathy*—more commonly referred to as "broken heart syndrome." According to the Mayo Clinic, this condition, also called *stress cardiomyopathy*, is a "heart condition brought on by stressful situations, such as the death of a loved one."[2] The clinic goes on to say that someone suffering from broken heart syndrome may experience sudden chest pain and suspect that he or she is having a heart attack, due to the heart's reaction to an influx of stress hormones in the body.

Earthquake Babies

After the devastating earthquake that shook Haiti in January 2010, I wanted to go down and pray for the people within six months of the disaster. Praise God, I was able to travel there less than four months after it happened. I prayed with the people, casting out the spirit of trauma from approximately 1.1 million individuals, and trained 700 pastors to do the same in their own congregations. We visited orphanages, hospitals, and nurseries where babies were being delivered in one big room, and we prayed over the newborns, casting out the trauma they had experienced from the earthquake, which had occurred while their mothers were still pregnant with them.

Just before the earthquake hit, arrangements had been made for some unborn babies to be adopted by American families. When these babies were between seven and nine months of age, reports starting coming in from their adoptive parents, saying, "We don't know what is going on with these babies. They are screaming in anger, raging, hitting us, biting, and demonstrating unbelievable hatred, and we don't know what to do." These parents were even considering sending the babies

---

[2]http://www.mayoclinic.com/health/broken-heart-syndrome/DS01135.

back to Haiti. Why were the babies acting this way? Because they had been traumatized while still in the womb.

Trauma Housed in the Heart

There was a woman who was having heart problems, and it came down to her needing a heart transplant. When she received the phone call informing her that a heart was ready for her, she was extremely excited. After the surgery, she stayed at the hospital, and, the first night, she had a horrific nightmare of being stabbed to death. This nightmare repeated itself for the following two nights, and her killer was the same person each time. So, the hospital contacted the police and brought them in to do a composite sketch of the person in her dream, according to her description. It ended up matching the features of the man who had murdered the person from whom she had received her new heart. That person had been stabbed to death, and that violent act was the last memory the person had experienced. The man was convicted of murder and is now in jail.

There was another lady who had a heart transplant and also was having recurring nightmares. Hers featured a license plate—the same number every night. The police were contacted and the plate number reported. Shortly thereafter, the police located the car and asked permission to search it. The driver said, "Sure, why not?" In the trunk, they found bloodstains which, when tested for DNA, matched the person whose heart the woman had received. The donor's uncle, who killed her, had thought she was already dead, and he'd thrown her in the trunk. As she was being shoved inside, she had seen the license plate, and the image of the number had been burned on her heart. That man was convicted and sentenced to time in prison.

That's the power of trauma. The same thing can happen to you. If your heart was transplanted in someone else, what kinds of trauma would that individual inherit? We're going to deal with the problem of trauma and more in this book.

We all experience traumatic experiences, to some degree. But we don't have to deal with the repercussions forever.

MY OWN TRAUMATIC EXPERIENCES

The Death of Both Parents

Within a span of two years, I lost both of my parents—my mother in 2009, my father in 2010. My mom passed away on a Tuesday morning, and I was told that my dad would be gone three to six days later.

On the eve of the fifth day, I was overcome with grief and trauma, which manifested physically by the loss of my voice. I was ministering out of town at the time and was scheduled to do a television show the next morning, for which I would need my full vocal capacity. So, I recognized that the spirits of trauma and grief were trespassing, and I determined that they would not remain in my body.

> *I recognized that the spirits of trauma and grief were trespassing, and I determined that they would not remain in my body.*

I went back to my hotel room, took a shower, and declared as loudly as I could, "In the name of Jesus, I curse this spirit of trauma—I curse this spirit of grief—and I command them to be gone. I command my voice to be completely restored, in Jesus' name." Then, I shouted, "Hallelujah!"

Not only were my vocal chords restored and my voice returned, but the heaviness of grief was lifted off of me. Plus, the Lord granted me additional time with my dad. I still missed my mom—don't misunderstand me—but the weight of grief left instantly. If I had not dealt with it immediately, I might not be here today, because the grief and trauma could have crippled me.

An Unsettling Phone Call

Before my husband, Kelley, started traveling full-time with Joan Hunter Ministries, he stayed at home, working and raising his four boys. One day, I called him on his cell phone, and an unfamiliar male voice answered. When he said, "Hello?" I said to myself, *No, not again. God, I don't want to go through this again. God, help me.* (You have to understand, prior to my marriage to Kelley, I was married to a man who was a homosexual. I couldn't bear the thought that Kelley might be having an affair with a man.) Fear gripped my heart, and I was speechless.

After a few moments of silence, the man on the phone said, "Do you want me to get my dad for you?" It was then that I recognized the voice and realized who it was: Kelley's son Kirk! I just wasn't accustomed to hearing his voice, which had gotten considerably lower in pitch because of puberty. Moreover, I wasn't aware that Kirk was staying at the house at the time.

When Kelley got on the phone, he wanted to know why I was crying. How could I tell him? I didn't until much later. It took a long time for me to come around and be comfortable explaining what had really happened. I was embarrassed that the thought would even cross my mind, because Kelley would never do something like that.

Nevertheless, I was a wreck. It had shocked me to the point of trauma to hear a man other than Kelley answer his cell phone. Some other ladies were traveling with me, and they insisted on praying with me. They told me to put my hand over my heart and to get rid of the trauma. I did, commanding that the spirit of trauma be gone, in Jesus' name. I knew I couldn't afford to let the emotional trauma fester, especially since my fears had been unfounded.

Chased by an Alligator

I'll give you another story of personal trauma from my childhood. I was born and raised in the Miami area, and we lived really close to the Miami Serpentarium, a tourist attraction where the founder, Bill Haast, would extract venom from snakes while visitors watched. Bill's daughter, Naia, went to school with me, and we sometimes got together to play. Every time I went to visit Naia, I got to see the reptiles, since her family lived in the back of the same building that housed the Serpentarium.

One day, we were playing—having "tea," if I remember correctly—and an alligator got loose and came after us. Alligators are fast, and they're a lot bigger than they look on television. So, here I am, this little six-year-old, trying to outrun an eight-foot alligator that's chasing me and my friend. Scared beyond words, Naia and I rushed into her bedroom and slammed the door behind us. That concluded my trauma related to alligators—or so I thought. As it turned out, it was only chapter one.

A few years ago, I attended a book convention in Orlando, Florida. Alligators are commonplace there, and I was not surprised when a voice announced over the loudspeakers that there was an "alligator on the floor." But I couldn't get the image of that eight-foot alligator at Naia Haast's house out of my mind. Nor could I stop picturing him chasing me again. Others were traveling with me, including my stepson Curtis. I said to him, "Look for the alligator, Curtis. Find the alligator. It's got to be somewhere around here." I wanted to find it before it found me.

Finally, we learned that the announcement had been a publicity stunt; there was a booth with a baby alligator, only about four feet long, whose mouth had been fastened shut. The alligator's keeper told me, "You can hold it if you want to." And I did! I couldn't believe how soft and smooth its tummy was. All of the fear and trauma had vanished!

THE DIFFERENCE BETWEEN TRAUMA AND GRIEF

When you are delivered from trauma, it doesn't mean that you forget the source of your grief—the loss of a loved one, for example— or that the experience will not cause you additional pain. That's not what I'm talking about. I miss being able to tell my mom, a well-known healing evangelist, about all of the incredible miracles that happen in my life. I miss sharing with her, for example, "I went to Haiti, Mom, and it was the biggest crusade our ministries have ever organized." I miss being able to talk to her. Everywhere I go, people tell me, "I got saved in one of your parents' services," or "I got the baptism of the Holy Ghost in one of your mom and dad's services." I missed her at my daughter's wedding. Every once in a while, I cry about things like that. But, please understand, my feelings are free from heaviness and trauma. There is a difference.

I want to remain completely free of trauma and unhealthy stress. And it's important for you to know, beyond a shadow of a doubt, that you, too, can remain trauma free! Situations will happen. Problems will arise. People you love will pass away. The longer you live, the more people you will see die. It's sad, but—praise God—I'm almost sixty years old, and I'm getting younger all the time.

DELIVERANCE IS POSSIBLE

We have the ability to break free from trauma through the power of God. Trauma is wreaking havoc in the bodies of countless people, and the only effective way of dealing with it is through prayer—through seeking the divine Physician. No human doctor has the ability to get inside our cells and scrape away all traces of the trauma. God alone has the power to do this.

One of the partners of 4 Corners Alliance, an apostolic group, had a friend in need of a kidney transplant. All of a sudden, a kidney became available, and she wondered why. Sure enough, there had been a horrendous murder the night before. She decided to lay hands on the container in which the kidney was being stored before the organ was put into her friend's body. As she did, she said, "I command that all traumas leave this kidney before it goes into my friend's body." It was a picture-perfect transplant, with minimal swelling and no infections whatsoever. The organ just "popped" in, almost as if God had performed the surgery. And there were no nightmares or other evidence of residual trauma or cellular memory.

This case, as well as the other cases of transplanted hearts mentioned earlier, has been documented and verified by the medical community. Let me reemphasize that trauma is real, and it isn't an experience that's merely metaphysical—it has physical implications. Trauma comes in and produces stress, which produces stress hormones, and these have the power to destroy the immune system if they are not dealt with properly—in other words, if they are not given over to God for healing.

TURN IT OVER TO GOD

When we turn our trauma over to God, He cleans out every cell with a "Holy-Ghost scalpel" and removes every ounce of trauma from our bodies. It works—hallelujah!

If you are praying for someone who has just come through a traumatic experience, say, "In the name of Jesus, I curse the spirit of trauma and command that it be gone. In Jesus' name, I command that any effect of the trauma be completely turned around and that this body be restored." Then, begin speaking the chemicals back into alignment; command the electrical and magnetic frequencies to go back into alignment. When you do that, it causes all kinds of things to be turned around and restored to their proper state.

My book *Healing the Whole Man Handbook* includes a chapter that deals with the electrical and magnetic frequencies in the human body.[3] In that chapter are prayers for the immune system. I pray for my immune system every day, saying something like this: "In the name of Jesus, I thank You that my immune system is doing what it is supposed to be doing."

As we discussed at the beginning of this chapter, our bodies' electrical and magnetic frequencies can be disrupted when traumatic "earthquakes" happen within our systems. Because of humanity's rebellion against God and subsequent fall, even when we haven't experienced trauma, we do not have the standard electrical and magnetic frequencies pulling on our bodies, as Adam and Eve originally had. There are people who wear magnetic necklaces, bracelets, shoes, soles, and other components in order to enhance their bodies' equilibrium. Some people say that this practice is of the devil. It's not of the devil; it's a legitimate method of helping to restore the body to its proper balance of electrical and magnetic frequencies.

I can command, in Jesus' name, that my body be in perfect harmony and balance, electrically and magnetically, without having to purchase expensive copper bracelets and such. I am not against these things, however.

RESTORE THE PROPER BALANCE

Those individuals with bipolar disorder have often experienced something traumatic that caused their bodies to be thrown off-kilter,

---

[3]Joan Hunter, *Healing the Whole Man Handbook* (New Kensington, PA: Whitaker House, 2005, 2006), 73–76.

chemically speaking. In these cases, it is necessary to curse the spirit of trauma and the spirit of bipolar disorder and to command the chemicals to return to harmony and balance.

To do this, place your hand on one side of your forehead and, as you move it from one side to the other, say, "In the name of Jesus, I remove the stigma of bipolar disorder." You should also curse any addictions to prescription medications.

Earthquakes can cause the planet to get off-kilter, and we need to do what we can to keep our bodies in proper balance. The body's pH is another area where balance is needed. When we experience stress, it produces acid, which causes our pH level to swing in one direction. It's important that we keep the proper amount of alkaline in our bodies, or the acid may cause ulcers or produce acid reflux. We must simply command our acid level to go down and our pH to return to its proper balance.

At a seminar where I was teaching, the organizers had everyone present take a pH test. Each of us was given a little spoon on which to put some of our spittle, as well as a piece of litmus paper, one type of pH indicator, to measure the alkaline and acidic levels of our saliva.

Next, each of us was given a small amount of fresh, undiluted lemon juice to swish around in our mouth, after which we tested our spittle yet again.

My results were normal the first time, and, only five minutes after I had filled my mouth with something that was highly acidic, my results were again normal—my body's pH had returned to its natural level in almost no time at all. Because of my strong immune system and low stress level, my pH measurement returned to normal extremely quickly. This was evidence of how well my body can handle stress. Some of the other people present were extremely stressed, and it was evident in the pH levels in their saliva.

It's amazing, but our spittle is one indicator of how our bodies handle stress. One lady testified, "Mine came back perfect, and it's because I read Joan Hunter's book *Power to Heal*." I responded, "Yes, praise God for bringing that pH balance back into alignment." I know what to do when stress comes on the scene—how to deal with it and get rid of it for good.

By the power of God, we can nip trauma in the bud. We can curse trauma and stress, as well as whatever brought them on: grief, loss, rejection, abuse, and so forth. We don't want to open the door to schizophrenia, bipolar disorder, agoraphobia, depression, fibromyalgia, a suppressed immune system, or anything of that nature. And this is one reason why we strive to get to the root of the problem before it grows into something disproportionately big.

> *We can curse trauma and stress, as well as whatever brought them on: grief, loss, rejection, abuse, and so forth.*

Depression plunges many people into a bipolar personality disorder or chronic fatigue. For them, getting out of bed can be the most difficult thing to do. Romans 13:11 says, *"And do this, knowing the time, that now it is high time to awake out of sleep* [out of depression]; *for now our salvation is nearer than when we first believed"* (NKJV).

It is now time to *"awake"* from depression. As Christians, we have hope in Jesus Christ. Someone may protest and say, "If you only knew why I am depressed." That's exactly why I am talking to you right now. It doesn't matter what occurred to cause your depression, your grief, your trauma, or your stress. What matters is that you allow the blood of Jesus to comfort you, cleanse you, and heal you. And you can do this only as you release whatever it is that brought about your depression, handing it over to Jesus to deal with.

DELIVERED FROM TRAUMA

By cursing the trauma and turning it over to God, countless people have broken free from the bondage of pain and launched new lives in freedom. The following are just a few examples to serve as inspiration and encouragement. You, too, can be delivered from trauma!

A Woman Healed of Childhood Trauma

I was ministering in Canada when a woman came up to me and said, "I want you to pray for me." I said, "Okay, no problem." She went on to explain that when she was a young girl, her parents placed her in an orphanage. The institution ran out of cribs, so, when she was two or three, she was sleeping in a "big girl" bed. Without any bars to keep her in, she had a tendency to get up out of bed and wander around. The staff at the orphanage wanted to keep her in the bed, and so they put her in a straightjacket and strapped her to the bed. She had to wait until morning to go to the bathroom.

As you can imagine, the experience was traumatic. So, here she was, extremely traumatized. I asked her to cross her arms over her chest, as if she were in a straightjacket. "I can't! I can't!" she screamed. I said, "If you'll give me about three minutes, you will be completely free." She said, "Okay, okay, okay," and she managed to place her hands across her chest. Then, I told her that I was going to squeeze her really tight, and she would be free. I used my arms like the straps of a straightjacket and held her really tight as I said, "In the name of Jesus, I curse this spirit of trauma and fear, and I command it to go in Jesus' name." I released my hands, and she crumpled to the floor. Moments later, she got up and said, "It's gone! It's gone!"

For years, she hadn't been able to be hugged by her husband. Now that she was free, she could go home and embrace him with open arms and without any fear. Hallelujah!

A Star Swimmer Regains His Winning Streak

My friend Debby Fry Wilson sent me the following testimony about her son.

In February 2011, my son, Hunter, was swimming in the Washington State high school championships. We were very hopeful because the year before, as a ninth grader, he was one of only a handful of freshmen to make finals at the state championships. So, we went into the meet feeling very optimistic. And, indeed, in the preliminaries, he swam great and made the finals in all his events.

But, after Hunter swam his last event at prelims—his signature event, the 100-meter backstroke—we noticed he was doubled over on the pool deck, clutching his hand. Apparently, he had swum so fast that he'd smashed his hand into the wall of the pool on his finish.

The next day, Hunter was trying to warm up for finals, and he was in so much pain that we rushed him to the emergency room. The doctor said he had a hairline rotated fracture from the base of his index finger to the top of his hand.

The problem was that in a couple of hours, he had to swim in two individual finals, as well as in the team medley relay final, an event in which the team was ranked in the top three in the state. He could give up his individual events, but if he didn't swim the medley relay, his relay team—three other boys and himself—would have to give up their big opportunity at the state championships.

The doctor said that if Hunter decided to swim, he chanced completely separating the fracture and might require surgery. He offered to tape Hunter's hand to help.

We prayed for a miracle and put our faith in God.

Hunter jumped in the water and did the underwater pullout on his leg of the medley relay—breaststroke—and, in that movement, he completely separated the bone. He later said he felt the bone completely crack apart and that the pain was excruciating. But Hunter kept swimming, and his relay team placed. He ultimately had to give up one of his individual events and managed to struggle through the other.

In the next couple of days, we learned of the severity of damage to Hunter's hand, which was more devastating than we'd thought possible. Hunter required surgery and had three screws permanently drilled into his hand bones to put it all back together.

In the last twelve months, we've watched Hunter struggle with swimming and noticed that he'll always be winning a backstroke race until the last twenty-five yards, only to lose in the last couple of yards—by a hair, even though he is fast enough to win these races and more.

A calendar year went by, and it was time again for the Washington State high school swimming championships. We all worried about what would happen there.

We had the revelation, based on Joan's teachings, that Hunter must have been traumatized by what happened to him and was afraid of hitting the wall again, so he was letting up on his finishes.

We texted Joan and asked for prayer for Hunter, and we followed her instructions and repeated the prayer over Hunter to curse all trauma and fear.

More importantly, we really released Hunter and his swimming career to the Lord. As much as we would have been thrilled to see Hunter win his events, we realized that we had to let go and let the Lord execute His own plan for Hunter.

In February 2012, Hunter swam the best swims of his life in prelims and in finals. Hunter swam fast enough to be recruited as a backstroker for NCAA division 1 in college and potentially to qualify for the U.S. Olympic trials in four years—and eventually more, if that is the Lord's plan for him.

We are so blessed to have the Lord answer our prayers over time and to give us revelations through Joan and her teachings. We know that Hunter's future, in swimming and in life, is in God's hands.

Feet Are Healed and Pain Is Gone

In Northern Ireland, a lady told me, "My feet hurt so bad. It's like walking on glass." But she didn't have a choice. She had to walk, since she had no wheelchair. Imagine every step you take feeling like broken glass piercing the soles of your feet. She also said that plenty of people had been praying for her, but to no avail. I asked her, "Has anyone prayed about your trauma?" She replied, "No." I asked her when her feet had started hurting. She said that, five years prior, she'd been in her car, and a street sweeper had come along and inadvertently picked up her car, carrying it down the street. She'd panicked because she couldn't get out of her car. So, she'd leaned back and used her feet to kick out the windshield. Glass had shattered everywhere, showering her as she climbed out, and her feet had recorded the trauma of that experience.

I said, "In the name of Jesus, I curse this trauma. I command it to be gone." Within seconds, she was saying, "Thank You, Jesus! Thank You, Jesus!" The pain was gone. When I'd met her, her ankles had been swollen over her shoes, which were at least one size too big to account for her inflamed feet. But, when we parted ways, she could barely keep the shoes on her feet due to how much the swelling had decreased.

No More Gagging

A woman came up for prayer when I was ministering in Myrtle Beach. She said, "I feel like I have something in the back of my throat. It's hard to swallow. I choke whenever I try to drink liquids." I said, "Okay, I will pray." She added, "I recently had surgery—a tongue reduction." I had never heard of such a procedure before. She went on, "I had a tongue reduction and a couple of other things on the inside of my mouth."

I soon found out that as she was coming out of the anesthesia, she kept repeating, "I can't breathe!" The nurses had assured her, "That's normal—you had a tube down your throat." She told them that it felt like she was being strangled, but they said, "It's just the anesthesia. Don't worry; it's a normal reaction." Still, she insisted, "I can't breathe." To pacify her, the nurses looked inside her mouth, and they found a piece of gauze they had stuffed there to soak up the blood from her tongue and had forgotten to remove. As a result, her tongue and throat were traumatized.

I said, "In the name of Jesus, I command all the trauma to go." The woman drank an entire glass of water without choking or gagging. It was the best glass of water she'd had in years.

Healed of Trichotillomania (Compulsive Hair-Pulling)

This powerful testimony comes from a young woman who is about to graduate from high school.

When I was in third grade (eight years old), I began to pull my hair out. Nobody knew why, and I don't even know how it happened. I just started pulling my hair out.

I didn't pull it out in chunks; I pulled my hair one at a time. By the time I was in fifth grade, I barely had any hair.

Kids would ask me if I had tried to cut my hair, and I would lie and tell them that's what I did. My parents had tried everything to get me to stop. They took me to a doctor, who had never seen anything like what I was doing; they prayed for me; they changed shampoos; they tried everything they could think of. Sometimes I would do better about not pulling, but I could never completely stop.

I hated pulling my hair. I felt like the ugliest person, and I hated myself because I couldn't stop. By the time I started my freshman year, I had given up hope that I would ever be able to stop, and I felt like I was the only one in the world with this problem. Then I met Kris Boston. She attends the same church I do, and she went up to my mom and asked if I pulled my hair out, because she did also. She had pulled for twenty years and desperately wanted to stop, like myself. I can't even explain how it feels to have somebody there for you who knows exactly what you're dealing with.

We began to send messages back and forth to each other. Then, in March 2009, Joan Hunter came to our church for special services. I was excited to go, and the first night was an awesome service, but I didn't go up to get prayed for. I was skeptical because I had been prayed for about pulling my hair many times before. Saturday night, during the entire service, I felt like I needed to get prayed for, and Kris came up to me near the end of the service and asked if I wanted to go with her after the service to have Joan pray for us. I said yes.

As soon as the service ended, we went and found Joan and explained our situations, and she prayed for us. She cursed the spirit of trauma, fear, and rejection. As soon as she began to pray for me, I felt a really warm feeling all over, and also the sense that a huge weight had been lifted off me. I felt happy; I wasn't even sure why. Kris told me she felt the same feelings come over her when she was prayed for. I knew when I got home that my struggle was over and I wouldn't pull my hair anymore. That was three years ago, and Kris and I both proudly have full heads of hair.

—*Maegan Jewell*

A Man with Schizophrenia Released to Minister Healing to Others

I met a man I'll call Frank who had been to a healing school. I prayed over him in Jesus' name and anointed him. The next day, I found out that he had been diagnosed with schizophrenia. I said, "That's easy," by which I meant that it was easy for God.

Schizophrenia is a condition that is brought on by trauma. Individuals with schizophrenia endured a trauma after which they formed a sort of shield around themselves—an alter ego or personality to hide behind, a wall that keeps them safe. Schizophrenics lead lonely lives, but at least other people leave them alone.

When I prayed for Frank again at the healing service, I said, "Father, in the name of Jesus, I curse this trauma, fear, abandonment, abuse, and rejection; I command it all to go. And I curse the spirit of schizophrenia, in Jesus' name, and I command the chemicals in this body to return to normal, in Jesus' name. Thank You, Jesus. Amen."

After the service, I asked Frank's pastors about the trauma he had experienced. I found out that when he was three years old, his mother had doused herself with gasoline and burned herself to death right in front of him. Upon her death, his father had gotten custody of the kids, and Frank's upbringing had been even more horrendous than watching his mother burn to death, if you can believe that. As a result, he'd built a shell to hide behind.

I had prayed for him on Sunday. The next day, he was back at the home where he lived, and he was doing well; plus, the church had been counseling him for five years. He was doing so well, they had provided him with toenail clippers, which is a big step in that home, and his job was to trim the toenails of other residents at the home. So, a man was lying on the table, waiting for Frank to clip his toenails, when Frank noticed that one of his legs was short. Frank asked him, "Do you have a back problem?" The man answered affirmatively. Frank prayed for him, and he was healed! Frank was so excited, he could hardly stand it. He wanted to pray for every person who needed healing.

A woman with a swollen ankle came limping down the hall. Up close, one could see that her ankle was a pretty shade of purple—pretty for fabric, that is. Frank said, "May I pray?" The woman responded, "Sure, what's it going to hurt?" He knelt down and prayed for her ankle. Within seconds, the ankle returned to its normal size and shade, and all the pain was gone.

Then, Frank went to church, where he was viewed by other people in one of two ways: *God can't use Frank because he has schizophrenia* or *If Frank can do it, I can do it, too!* Frank said, "I know Joan prayed for me, I know she laid hands on me, but I really, really didn't think God could use me." He was totally, completely set free from schizophrenia. Hallelujah!

Freed from the Trauma of Agoraphobia

There was a lady who came to a meeting in Florida, but she couldn't bring herself to come inside the church because she had agoraphobia, which is defined by *Merriam-Webster's 11th Collegiate Dictionary* as "abnormal fear of being helpless in an embarrassing or unescapable situation that is characterized especially by the avoidance of open or public places." So, she just sat in the foyer with her dog. The woman has a multimillion-dollar company, and one of her employees was a member of this church. This employee explained that her boss ran her business out of her home, where she felt safe; her conviction was that every time she would go out, something horrific would happen. What a lonely life! For protection, she took her dog along whenever she did venture out—to check the mail, for example. She never did anything by herself.

When she came to the church on that Friday night, I was informed that she was in the lobby, so I went out there and prayed for her. I cursed the spirit of trauma and fear and commanded the agoraphobia to go, in Jesus' name. On Sunday morning, she came back to the church, this time by herself! Hallelujah! She was totally free. What an awesome work of God!

Healed of Abandonment Issues

I was ministering at a church, and I said, "Who would like to be healed as a demonstration?" A lady came forward, and I started speaking to her, but she wouldn't make eye contact with me; she kept her focus on her husband, who was seated in the second or third row. I thought to myself, *This is not going to work*. Then, I turned her around so that she could no longer see her husband.

Yet, as I talked to her and asked her questions, she kept turning around! I thought, *What is going on here?* I soon found out that she had experienced the trauma of abandonment as a child, and, as a result, she feared that her husband would leave her, even while she was standing with me at the front of the church. They had been married for more than forty-five years, and he'd never left her, yet she was petrified that he would! Every morning when he left for work, she experienced a panic attack. Can you imagine leaving your wife while she's having a panic attack every workday for forty-five years? In public restrooms, she was stricken with fear and insisted that her husband stand just outside the door so that they could communicate, giving her reassurance that he was not going to leave her while she was in the restroom.

Talk about a controlling spirit of fear brought on by the trauma of abandonment and perpetuated by a dread of future abandonment! She could not handle it. He hadn't left her in over forty-five years, but she still couldn't shake the fear that he would leave her today. God bless that man!

I prayed for the spirit of trauma and abandonment to come out. A few days later, I received an e-mail from the woman. She said that they got up one morning, and her husband said, "Would you go to the local drugstore and get me a newspaper?" And she said, "Sure." She got in the car and drove to the store, only to find that it hadn't opened yet. While she was waiting, other cars pulled up in the parking lot. She knocked on the window of one of the cars and asked the driver, "May I pray for you while we are waiting?" And she did that to every other car in the lot. Then, when the store opened, she went inside, purchased a newspaper, and returned to her car. As she was driving home, she said to herself, "I'm really healed!" She had left her husband at home! A few months later, she was driving several hours to attend my meetings, all by herself. That's freedom.

Healed of Injuries Sustained in an Auto Accident

I prayed for a lady who had been in a car accident in which another car had T-boned hers. Although she had sustained no specific injuries, her body was in excruciating pain. I did not pray for her healing. Instead, I said, "In the name of Jesus, I command the trauma that the left side of this body is experiencing to go." Just like that, the trauma was gone, and so was the pain.

Beauty Restored by the Departure of Trauma

I prayed for another woman who had been in a terrible car accident that had destroyed her face at the age of fourteen. Her head had been propelled forward into the windshield. Thanks to skilled plastic surgeons, today, her face has no signs of scarring; she is absolutely beautiful. But her body had been so mangled that there was not a single place where she didn't hurt because of the trauma, and her body had contorted into the shape of the letter *C*. Everybody in her church had prayed for her. She had been told that she would never walk again, yet, today, she is a gorgeous, tall blonde. You would never guess that she had been in such a terrible accident. We prayed for the trauma to go and for her body to go back into alignment. Her hips had twisted and her collarbone had been broken, but we prayed for realignment, and her body ended up perfect.

After that, she said, "Only one thing: I feel like I have something right here." I put my hand over her face like a mask, to represent the impression caused by the impact of the windshield, and said, "Father, in the name of Jesus, I command that spirit of trauma to leave her face, and I command that mask to be taken off, in Jesus' name." And it was off. She'd felt like she'd had a clamp on her arm for many years, but she was set free when we cast off the spirit of trauma.

Sleeping Patterns Restored

I prayed for the leader of a church in Illinois who had not slept in a bed for more than four years—he'd slept only in chairs—and had incurred back injury as a result. Everyone in the church had prayed for him. I said, "In the name of Jesus, I command the spirit of trauma to go." Immediately, all of the pain and trauma left, and he has slept in his bed ever since.

TRAUMA IS SERIOUS

Trauma has a truly profound impact on the body. When I pray for people to get healed, the results are phenomenal, but when I pray and cast out the spirit of trauma, it propels people to an entirely new level of deliverance. I have been praying this way for many, many years, but I am bringing it to the forefront now because I am seeing the effects of trauma manifest in people's lives more noticeably than ever before.

> *Jesus Christ bears our burdens and makes everything easier.*

We need to get rid of the trauma. The process truly is easier than most people might imagine, especially for those whose hope is in Jesus Christ. He bears our burdens and makes everything easier. He says to each of us, *"Come to me, all you who are weary and burdened, and I will give you rest"* (Matthew 11:28).

PRAYER FOR RELEASE FROM TRAUMA

It's time to get rid of all of the trauma in your life, whether it was caused by an alligator, a car accident, childhood abuse, or something else. Some of you were molested as children. That was traumatic. Some of you were verbally abused by a parent or a teacher. That was traumatic. Some of you have been traumatized by divorce or the loss of a loved one. One simple prayer, below, will cover it all. But I encourage you, after today, to pray over yourself again to be more specific. If I were praying for myself, I'd name the trauma of being chased by an alligator, the trauma of being abandoned by my natural father, and the trauma of being molested by an uncle. Some traumas you may not even be aware of until you get the opportunity to deal with something similar again.

I want you to place your hands over your heart and receive this prayer: "Father, right now, in the name of Jesus, I send the word of healing to each person reading this book. Father, right now, in the name of Jesus, I curse the spirit of trauma and command it to be gone. I curse any feelings of abandonment, of rejection, of abuse, and of worthlessness; I command every bit of that to go. I curse any spirits of hopelessness, depression, and oppression, and I command those to be gone, in Jesus' name. I speak life, health, wholeness, and complete restoration into the life of this person, and I command all of the chemicals to be returned to their proper balance, in Jesus' name. Amen."

When you have been freed from trauma, you will find that some of the ailments you were suffering from have gone, as well, because they were caused by trauma.

Scriptures to Take to Heart

Then they cried out to the Lord in their trouble, and He saved them out of their distresses. (Psalm 107:19 NKJV)

You are my hiding place; you will protect me from trouble and surround me with songs of deliverance. (Psalm 32:7)

[Jesus said,] *"Come to me, all you who are weary and burdened, and I will give you rest. Take my yoke upon you and learn from me, for I am gentle and humble in heart, and you will find rest for your souls. For my yoke is easy and my burden is light."* (Matthew 11:28–30)

CHAPTER 2

Stress Has Serious Consequences

Did you know that the stress we experience isn't just in our thoughts and emotions? Like trauma, stress has a lot of power. It can cause acid reflux disease, irritable bowel syndrome, Crohn's disease, heart attacks, strokes, diabetes, and ulcers, to name just a few of its physical consequences. It also affects our height and our posture. Many times, when I have prayed for people to be healed of stress and trauma, their bodies have grown, and their necks and shoulders have straightened. When trauma leaves, the body is able to return to its natural height.

WHEN TRAUMA TURNS INTO STRESS

This is the progression that typically occurs after a traumatic experience. The trauma brings about stress, which suppresses the immune system. If the immune system remains suppressed, illness can take hold, and prolonged sickness often leads to hopelessness. If a state of hopelessness is not remedied, it turns into depression, which may, in turn, cause stress syndrome, fibromyalgia, or chronic fatigue syndrome.

As if all of this were not enough, these final stages may lead to suicide for those who feel there is no other way to deal with their problems. Many people believe they would rather be dead than live with all of the pain and heartache they're feeling.

But that's not what we want! We want to nip trauma in the bud. Again, when my mom died, I was hit with grief and trauma, but I dealt with them before they could progress into chronic illness. When I lost my voice because I was experiencing a heaviness that was almost unbearable, I laid my hands on my heart and cursed the spirits of trauma and grief, commanding them to go. They were trespassing on God's property! Then, I commanded my voice to come back, and I said, "Hallelujah!" as loudly as I could.

When you trust in the Lord, you can lay hands on yourself and command that the spirit of trauma depart, in Jesus' name.

Today, I'm healthy. When my dad died, I again put my hands on my own heart and prayed. It's okay if my husband and I stand in agreement for deliverance or if I have a ministry partner agree with me in prayer, but I can also lay hands on myself and command the trauma to depart. In the same way, you don't have to come to me or seek another healing minister for deliverance from trauma. When you trust in the Lord, you can lay hands on yourself and command that the spirit of trauma depart, in Jesus' name.

THE TRUE MEANING OF STRESS

While giving a presentation on stress management, a speaker walked around the room carrying a glass of water. Everyone was expecting her to ask whether they would describe the glass as being half empty or half full. But she threw them for a loop by saying, "How heavy is this glass of water?"

The group began to call out guesses ranging from 8 ounces to 20 ounces.

When the group had quieted again, the speaker replied, "The absolute weight doesn't matter. It all depends on how long I hold it. If I hold it for a minute, that's not a problem. If I hold it for an hour, I'll have an ache in my right arm. If I hold it for a day, you'll have to call an ambulance for me. In each case, it's the same weight, but, the longer I hold it, the heavier it becomes." She continued, "That's the way it is with stress. If we carry our burdens all the time, sooner or later, as the burdens become increasingly heavy, we won't be able to carry on.

No matter what you're carrying, you have to set it down and rest awhile before you take it up again. When you've been refreshed, you can carry on. As early in the evening as you can, put all your burdens down. Don't carry them through the evening and into the night. Whatever burdens you're carrying now, lay them down. Relax and give them to God.

ESCAPE THE MIND-SET OF DENIAL

A state of denial will counteract all of our efforts to rid ourselves of harmful stress. To demonstrate this at a seminar, I asked for a volunteer, and a woman named Vivian came up to help me. The demonstration involved my asking her a series of questions and her responding to them.

Here is a rundown of how it went:

Me: "Are you married?"

Vivian: "Yes, I am."

Me: "And have you been married before?"

Vivian: "Yes, I have."

(I told her to put out one hand to represent what she was carrying. Then, I put a big dictionary on it to symbolize carrying her husband, followed by another dictionary to represent carrying her ex-husband. Then, I resumed my questioning.)

Me: "Do you have children?"

Vivian: "Yes."

Me: "How many children do you have?"

Vivian: "Altogether, six."

(You know what I did next. Yes, I added six more books— medium-sized ones, mind you.)

Me: "Are your children married?"

Vivian: "Yes, two are."

I added two more books.

Me: "Are any of them divorced?"

Vivian: "No."

Me: "Grandchildren?"

Vivian: "Ah, yes."

Me: "Are you going to tell me how many?"

Vivian: "Two."

Me: "Two so far." I added two more books. "How are your finances?"

Vivian: "They could be better."

(I added another book.)

Me: "How is your health?"

Vivian: "Could be better."

(Another book.)

Me: "Are your mom and dad still alive?"

Vivian: "Yes."

Me: "Are they in good health?"

Vivian: "No."

(Two more books.)

Me: "How is your relationship with your husband?"

Vivian: "Good."

Me: "Everything is going well with your children who are married and everything else?"

Vivian: "Everything is great."

Me: "Everything is great?"

By this time, the weight and burden of the books was obviously causing a strain. Vivian's countenance had changed; her posture was crumbling; and her stress level had increased.

The normal response from most women is, "Everything is great; I can do this, no matter what." No one wants to admit defeat especially when family responsibilities are concerned. However, your body, mind, and emotions can only handle so much. Somewhere along the line, something is going to happen. Some won't give up until sickness, disease, or injury sideline them. With others, it may take a complete emotional breakdown.

It is impossible to truly understand the strain you are feeling until it is lifted off your shoulders. You will find it is amazing how much weight you unconsciously bear on your shoulders.

Everyone has a choice. You can continue to carry the load that is way too heavy for you or you can get rid of the burdens of life by giving them away. Willing hands and a giant heart are waiting to carry everything for you. Your Father offers to take them. You don't have to handle 50 percent or 40 percent or even 5 percent of the burden while He carries the rest. You can freely lay every single large book or concern or burden at His feet.

Why do you want to carry all those problems when He not only will handle them, but He also knows the best way to resolve the situations? God will respect your decision, one way or the other. He will let you carry the weight until you are prepared to admit that you can't make it without Him. You have the choice to give it all to Him or to hold on to everything yourself.

Some drop the load; some add on to the load, even though the "books" they are carrying weigh more than they do. God wants to take every burden off your shoulders. The key is this: You must let Him! Release your burdens to Him. Place every problem on His altar. He will take care of everything for you. He is waiting for you.

ELIMINATE STRESS THROUGH RELEASING

First Peter 5:7 says, *"Let* [God] *have all your worries and cares, for he is always thinking about you and watching everything that concerns you"* (TLB). It's important to remember that nothing is ever *altered* until we lay it on the *altar*.

I can't carry the weight of my husband on my shoulders—worrying about what he's doing, wondering what he's up to. I especially can't carry that weight in addition to the weight of eight children, four grandchildren, many ministry employees, my financial responsibilities, and so on. It's exhausting—not to mention impossible! Believe it or not, I do sleep. And I don't have to worry because I've laid everything on the altar. It's amazing how light your load becomes once you've done that.

PLACE YOUR LOVED ONES ON GOD'S ALTAR

In 2000, after my divorce was final, my ex-husband called and asked to take our daughters out to dinner. Melody was away on a missions trip, and another daughter was out of town, so there were two daughters at home. I encouraged them to go, because I felt it was important for them to continue having a relationship with their dad. And so, when he called and asked my daughters if they would like to go out for dinner, it was fine with me—financially, things were tight, and that meant two meals I wouldn't have to pay for.

He took them out to eat at a really nice restaurant. Afterward, he told them, "The night is young. Let's go out and do something else." Hours later, they finally came home. When they walked in the door, I asked them, "Where have you been?" They said, "Oh, Dad took us out to a lesbian bar and gave us all the drinks we wanted." One of them wasn't even of drinking age! Talk about anger. I was so mad at him. I couldn't believe it. Then, the next night, they got together with their dad again—and he took them to another lesbian bar! And, again, they came home smelling of alcohol. I was so upset. When they got home, I was waiting. Emphatically, I told them, "This is not the way you were raised. You know better than this. You are adult children; you know what you are supposed to do and what you are not supposed to do." My ex-husband wanted to portray his gay/lesbian lifestyle as normal. Although God loves people who are living a homosexual lifestyle, He hates homosexuality and any kind of fornication.

The third time my daughters went out with their dad, I'd had it. When they came in, I said, "I can't believe you have done this," and I added a few more words of disapproval. Then, I went to my bedroom, shut the door, got in the shower, and started crying out to God, saying, "God, I can't fix these girls. I have done everything I know to do, and I can't fix them." I was fit to be tied—I was so mad! And I'll never forget what God said to me: "Duh!" He wanted to make sure I understood Him. Then, I told Him, "I give

When we put our children on God's altar, He turns their lives around. I've experienced it firsthand.

them to You." And in His still, small voice, He said, "I've been waiting on you to do this. You've gotten in the way of Me and My Holy Spirit where your girls are concerned." I repented and put them on the altar.

The next night, they came home from an evening out with their dad. This time, I embraced them instead of yelling. Then, I went to my bedroom, shut the door, and got in the shower, where I said to God, "Did You see what Your daughters did?" I wasn't responsible anymore; I had placed them on His altar.

They never went out with their dad to the gay bars again. God proved He could do a better job than I could!

When we put our children on God's altar, He turns their lives around. I've experienced it firsthand. Let God take care of them. He'll do a better job than any of us can ever hope to do. But we need to place them on His altar.

If you are a married woman, I'm sure you've made at least one honest attempt to "fix" your husband. All of us have. We get married, and we think we'll make our husbands into who we want them to be. But the important thing is that they become who *God* wants them to be. Men really are smarter than women—two weeks into the marriage, they give up trying to fix their wives, realizing it's impossible, whereas we women will "die trying." We believe it's within our being to fix things—our spouse, our children, everything. Women are "fix-it" people! But if we're doing all of the "fixing," God can't do His part.

That's why we need to place our spouses on God's altar along with our children. If you're not sure whether you've done this, rest assured that you'll go through a test within twenty-four hours. Something will come up—your children will act out, your husband will say something insensitive—and your response will indicate whether or not you have placed them successfully on God's altar.

If you find that you did, indeed, place them on the altar, forgive them and leave them there. If you go and get them off of the altar, you are trespassing on God's property. Leave them there and let the Lord deal with them! He knows how to crank up the fire. Trust Him to know how much He needs to raise the temperature.

I love my niece and nephew, but if something were to happen to them, I would be involved at a distance, praying and interceding on their behalf. However, if something were to happen to one of my own children, my inclination would be to step in immediately. We need to think about how we would react to our nieces and nephews when we react to our children, because that kind of response indicates that we've placed them on the altar. They are truly God's.

If you are a married man, I am going to lead you in a prayer. Husbands, you will place your wife (or future wife) on the altar.

"Father, I lay my wife on the altar. I can't fix her. You know I've tried. I release her to You. Show me how to be a better husband."

Now, the wives:

"Father, I lay my husband (present or future) on the altar. I can't fix him. God, You know I've tried! So, I lay him on the altar. I release him to You. Father, show me how to be a better wife."

And everybody, together:

"Father, bless our marriage. Amen."

I have gotten free of trauma, and so can you. I have gotten free of having to carry the weight of the ministry. I know I can't carry the ministry on my own or generate the funds to keep it functioning. I do my part, and God does His. It's phenomenal what He can do. I have four daughters, and, even though they are already on God's altar, I remind Him through prayer of their position there. I remind Him that it's His job to take care of them, and I still pray for them. It is awesome to watch Him work in their lives. My daughters have been transformed. I can't even begin to tell what has happened in the family because of my children.

Hallelujah! Let's move on to our children. Place them on God's altar, one at a time, with the following prayer:

"Father, I thank You for _____(the name of the son or daughter you're praying for). I release _____to You and lay him/her on Your altar. I release him/her to You. Show me how to be a better mom/dad. In Jesus' name, amen."

Hallelujah!

Let's close with a Scripture from Isaiah:

But thus saith the L*ord, Even the captives of the mighty shall be taken away, and the prey of the terrible shall be delivered: for I will contend with him that contendeth with thee, and I will save thy children.*

(Isaiah 49:25 KJV)

God promises to save your children—that's His responsibility. Our responsibility, as moms and dads, is to love them. To correct them gently, not to condemn them. When we parent in this way, our children will seek our advice on their own rather than resenting it and willfully rebelling against it. They will call and ask us, "What should I do in this situation?" In these cases, I never tell my children what to do, because I know that if I say the wrong thing, they'll blame me. They are old enough to make decisions for themselves.

All we need to do as parents is to point them to the Bible—God's Word—and to share any insights the Lord gives to us into their situation. Sometimes, He speaks to my spirit, and I am able to prophesy over my children. Every prophetic word I have spoken over my children has come to pass. When we give them over to God, we need to truly let them be His.

Understand that it is not our responsibility, as parents, to save our children. That's a decision they need to make for themselves, through the prompting of the Holy Spirit. Our job is to love them unconditionally. To do this effectively, we need to place them on the altar.

It's overwhelming when I think about everything I could be shouldering by myself: my husband, my children, my grandchildren, my in-laws, my employees, my pastor, my ministry partners, and so forth. But, praise God, I've placed all of those people on the altar! I have a lot of responsibilities, but I never struggle with the heaviness of stress, and I thank God for that.

I want to encourage you to take the steps to free your body of trauma and stress. Again, once you do, some of the diseases and discomforts brought on by the trauma will subside, either instantly or over a period of time. One thing is certain: the level of pain you experience will go down immediately. You will start to feel the release of stress in your neck, shoulders, and back. When you reach that point, you will know that everything concerning you has been placed on God's altar.

In the next chapter, my daughter Spice is going to give us a closer look at the impact of stress on the human body, as well as what we can do to prevent it.

Scriptures to Take to Heart

You will keep him in perfect peace, whose mind is stayed on You, because he trusts in You.   (Isaiah 26:3 NKJV)

Anxiety in the heart of man causes depression, but a good word makes it glad.   (Proverbs 12:25 NKJV)

Who of you by worrying can add a single hour to his life?
                                              (Matthew 6:27; Luke 12:25)

Finally, brethren, whatever things are true, whatever things are noble, whatever things are just, whatever things are pure, whatever things are lovely, whatever things are of good report, if there is any virtue and if there is anything praiseworthy; meditate on these things.
                                              (Philippians 4:8 NKJV)

CHAPTER 3

Wired but Tired

My daughter Spice A. Lussier, NMD, is a licensed physician of naturopathic medicine. She operates a clinic in the Phoenix, Arizona, area, where she specializes in treating the whole man with an emphasis on botanical medicine, homeopathy, acupuncture, and nutritional supplementation. Her goal is to treat the root cause, not just the symptoms, of whatever is ailing her patients.

She graduated from Oral Roberts University with a Bachelor of Science in biomedical chemistry. Upon completing her degree, she took a job as a receptionist at an HMO (health maintenance organization), where she was awakened to the impersonal, businesslike approach of many doctors to treating their patients. The pattern of five-minute evaluations, followed by the dispensing of a prescription drug, spurred her desire to go into medicine—but with a different approach. At that time, she'll tell you, her idea of disease prevention was to take a multivitamin every day. She hadn't heard of naturopathic medicine, much less studied it. A friend of hers who worked at the HMO suggested she look into a program at the Southwestern College of Naturopathic Medicine & Health Sciences, located in Arizona. She went to visit the school, and the rest is history.

She supplied the following material, based on her expertise and experience.

•••

Let's play a little guessing game. Can you guess what organ I am? I come in a pair, each part weighing less than 2 ounces each; I'm shaped like a triangle; I'm the largest I'll ever be when I'm inside a seven-month-old fetus; I get smaller and smaller over the course of a lifetime. I control sleep, blood pressure, blood sugar, and your response to stress. That's a lot to do for something so tiny, right?

I'm the adrenal glands. These glands are two tiny organs involved in the symphony that is the endocrine system, which comprises the thyroid gland, the thymus, the pancreas, the ovaries/testes, and the adrenal glands. The adrenal glands are located right above your kidneys at the back of your body. Each of them is an intricate organ that produces chemicals that work in harmony with one another.

When patients come to me complaining of fatigue, stress, and other problems, they often blame their thyroid or a hormonal imbalance due to menopause, for example. They fail to realize that it very well could be the result of overworking their adrenal glands, which often get overlooked because of their small size and seemingly minor importance.

Each adrenal gland weighs between four and six grams and is only about five centimeters by two centimeters in size. Yet they have a huge job to do: they produce multitudes of different hormones, one of which is adrenaline. A casual definition of *adrenaline* is the rush that you feel when you're about to rear-end the car in front of you, when a deer or other animal darts out in front of your car, when you're running away from a bear, or when you're doing something equally stimulating. Adrenaline has a more technical name: *epinephrine*. We have this sympathomimetic hormone in our systems as a survival chemical, of sorts. It's the hormone that kicks in when you know you aren't strong enough to lift a car until someone is trapped underneath and then you do. It builds our muscle, boosts our energy, and bolsters our strength—all good, healthy things that should happen on a normal basis.

Cortisol is another hormone secreted by the adrenal glands. It's our long-acting stress hormone. Cortisol is also important in our sleep-wake cycles; it gives us a boost in the morning and, ideally, carries us throughout the day.

Testosterone is an important hormone that is reduced through menopause, which is why many menopausal women experience low libido—a lack of sexual desire. Thus, it's important for our adrenal glands to be functioning properly.

DHEA is a prohormone (a precursor of a hormone) that acts as a building block for all of the sex hormones, primarily estrogen, testosterone, and progesterone.

The last hormone is aldosterone, which is important for blood pressure regulation. Blood pressure problems—too high or too low—plague a lot of people. Perfect harmony is the goal.

Let's look more closely now at how the functions and effects of the hormones at work in our bodies. Adrenaline is also a neurotransmitter—a chemical that regulates numerous physical and emotional processes. Specifically, adrenaline produces the "fight or flight" response. Another neurotransmitter is histamine, which helps to control our sleep-wake cycles and also produces anti-inflammatory chemicals.

Often, I see people with adrenal problems that manifest as inflammation in several areas—their digestive tract, their skin, and so forth. Adrenal problems can also cause your blood sugar level to spike, which is a good thing if you can't find food but a bad thing if you have no way to control that blood sugar.

Cortisol should be high in the morning—say, between seven and noon—and it should drop significantly in the afternoon. You should get just a little bump for that afternoon energy burst, and then at night it should be very low, because that corresponds with your sleep-wake cycle. In the morning, it gives you the "get up and go" that you need. Again, in the afternoon, it should cycle a little bit, kind of like a kick to get us going through the rest of the evening.

Adrenal fatigue is not recognized as an ailment by most medical doctors, and so it is neither diagnosed nor treated. If you walk into your doctor's office tomorrow and say, "I have adrenal fatigue," he very well may laugh. This condition is one you'll want to consult a naturopathic doctor or natural health care provider about. So many people suffer from being what I call "wired but tired." They lead busy lives and feel as if they're getting a lot accomplished, yet they're exhausted at the same time; they aren't sleeping at night. It's a broad spectrum of symptoms: at one end, you can just be overly tired—more than you ought to be, considering your activity level. You can even feel nervous and jittery throughout the day without knowing why. You may even wonder, "Why am I feeling this way? I haven't had more than a cup of coffee or two." At the other end of the spectrum—at the extreme—you can experience burnout that leads to depression.

Insomnia is a major aspect of being "wired but tired." So are cravings for sweet and/or salty foods. This is because the adrenal glands control our blood sugar and our blood pressure, and we will crave sugar or salt, respectively, to boost our blood sugar or to increase our blood pressure if our adrenal glands aren't functioning properly.

Heart palpitations and poor digestion are additional symptoms of this imbalance, the reason being that we are constantly in "fight or flight" mode, due to the signals our adrenal glands are sending, and we are unable to benefit from the other aspect of our nervous system, which offers rest and digestion. So, if we are constantly busy and stressed— if we are living in "fight or flight" mode—we lose the ability to rest and digest, and our digestive systems can actually start breaking down, leading to such ailments as ulcers, irritable bowel syndrome (IBS), and constipation.

Then, there are allergies, which flare up when our immune system reacts to our environment. In a similar way, some people experience skin rashes and/or eczema. It wasn't until I first studied adrenal fatigue that I understood how it related to inflammation and poor digestive health.

Our bodies don't know the difference between real stress and perceived stress; they react the same way to both.

What are the influences that negatively affect our adrenal glands and cause them to get "out of whack," so to speak? In the first place, one of the biggest factors is stress, whether it's real—the stress we experience in a fast-paced, deadline-driven work environment, for example—or perceived—the worry that we invite into our minds when we compare ourselves to others, dwell on financial issues, or otherwise impose psychological stressors on ourselves. Our bodies don't know the difference between real stress and perceived stress; they react the same way to both. And that is something that's important to focus on: not dwelling on these stressful ideas, because we're essentially inviting the same stress as we might experience in a high-pressure job or while running a marathon.

Next is a lack of sleep and adequate exercise. How many people get the recommended nine hours of uninterrupted sleep every night? How many people exercise for two-and-a-half hours a day? It's hard to do, but it gives us a way to release our stress and helps to regulate our sleep. A lack of exercise, on the other hand, can contribute to our stress. So can skipping meals. How many of us go through our day, suddenly realize we're starving, and then remember that we never ate breakfast or lunch? We burn through all of the stored sugar that our liver has in reserve, and then, when that has been consumed, the liver signals the adrenal glands to secrete hormones that raise our blood sugar because we haven't eaten. That isn't a desirable function, however, because it signals our bodies to eat rather than to draw from the energy we have stored away.

A third factor is a vitamin deficiency. The adrenal glands have an amazing ability to use the vitamins C and B—vitamin B-5, in particular. Granted, most people are not B-5 deficient, because it is readily available in many different foods. Another name for this vitamin is pantothenic acid, and the prefix "pan-" means "everywhere." However, stress can deplete your supply of B-5, making you deficient in this vitamin. And if you're stressed, often times, you aren't eating a balanced diet. You can burn through your B-5 pretty quickly, and your adrenal glands will suffer as a result.

It's similar with vitamin C. During periods of stress, your body needs more vitamin C. People think of vitamin C as something to take when you have a cold or flu, and I would absolutely encourage that, in a daily dose of three to six grams, whether you're battling illness, infection, and stress or not. Again, it's to protect those small, delicate adrenal glands.

As I mentioned earlier, there is a symphony going on among the various organs of the endocrine system. If you have diabetes, which is a disorder of the pancreas, or if you have hypothyroidism that is not being managed well, it can place an undue burden on the adrenal glands because the organs are all trying to help each other out. And some will be more burdened than others at different stages of life. A major such stage is when a woman reaches menopause (as well as if she has a hysterectomy). In this process, there is a shift of hormonal production from the ovaries to the adrenal glands, which are more heavily burdened as a result. So, if you have spent your adulthood working a very busy job and taking care of your family—burning the candle at both ends—and then you go through menopause, you may wonder why you are getting various physical symptoms all of a sudden. It's because there's supposed to be a natural shift of work duty from the ovaries to the adrenal glands. But if you've already tapped those out during your first fifty years of life, they are not going to be there for you. So, it's very important to nurture them. Support your entire hormonal system, especially when you are going through menopause.

THREE STAGES OF HORMONAL BURNOUT

Hormonal burnout does not happen overnight. It's the result of a gradual process by which stress attacks us. There are three different phases in the operation of the adrenal glands in relation to hormonal burnout: functional; then, adapting; then, dysfunctional. The first phase is the alarm phase, and it's brought on by acute stress that, in many cases, stems from natural, everyday occurrences and is completely warranted. In this phase are such actions as running away from a bear or swerving to avoid an accident while driving. Then, there is the resistance stage, which is the state of chronic, long-term stress, either real or perceived, which leads to the decreased functioning of the adrenal glands. Then comes the phase of burnout and collapse. This is the phase that sends celebrities to the hospitals to be treated for "exhaustion." We read about these instances in the tabloids, and, whether the diagnosis is a cover-up or not, there is a legitimate medical condition that results from going and going until there comes a moment when you simply cannot get out of bed. I have treated people who have reached this point—finally, their bodies said, "No more."

Our goal is to prevent ourselves from reaching that point.

Phase 1: Alarm

In the first phase, the adrenal glands are secreting cortisol and epinephrine as a natural reaction to stress, real or perceived. This is a normal reaction. After such an event, recovery takes between twenty-four and forty-eight hours. When this happens to you, make sure you allow yourself time to recover! If we don't react to it, and if we're constantly going through this cycle of acute stress, it can lead to chronic anxiety because our bodies are so quick to jump into "fight or flight" mode, even at the smallest, most mundane of triggers. During my four years in medical school, I experienced chronic stress to the extent that I became extremely jumpy; a door slamming shut in my apartment building would make me leap a mile. But it wasn't legitimate anxiety.

Again, you can experience anxiety as a symptom of adrenal gland deficiency, and it's important to get to the bottom of the root cause of all anxiety.

> *You can experience anxiety as a symptom of adrenal gland deficiency, and it's important to get to the bottom of the root cause of all anxiety.*

In a regular sleep-wake cycle, cortisol levels are to be high in the morning. Yet, for some people, it's flipped; their bodies don't know which end is up because they are dealing with constant stress that may lead to sleep disorders. It may also contribute to gastric ulcers, which result because being in "fight or flight" mode suppresses our inclinations to rest and digest. Our bodies put a halt on saliva production, which can eventually cause tooth decay, because one purpose of saliva is to "bathe" the teeth and wash away all of the bacteria that resides in the mouth. Saliva is also the first step in digestion—it begins to break down the food we eat while it's in our mouths. Our stomachs are supposed to produce mucus that helps protect the stomach lining from the acid, and problems result when this does not happen properly. It can lead to a feeling of intestinal irritation. You may be popping antacids, not really knowing what is going on. Your discomfort may be a result of the alarm phase of adrenal reaction or of adrenal exhaustion. Cortisol suppresses the immune system, as well. It acts as an anti-inflammatory, but it also lowers our immunity to "bugs" and nasty viruses and parasites and that sort of thing. Thus, frequent infections are another symptom of adrenal fatigue.

Phase 2: Resistance

The second phase, which is the resistance phase, is where most of us live. It's characterized by chronic stress over long periods of time—even stress that's merely perceived. Cortisol and epinephrine are still at work; your adrenal glands are pumping out these hormones at a high rate. It's doing its thing, and you're wondering, "When am I going to get a break?" When someone shows me his or her appointment book and tells me how busy life is, my adrenal fatigue radar goes off. While it's good to be involved in worthwhile activities, it still puts a burden on your glands. This is often when weight gain starts, usually in the abdominal region. And I believe this is because the adrenal glands need to be able to draw on fuel. So, they're anticipating the famine they assume is coming, based on the way you've been feeling stressed and failing to digest properly. That why those hormones are in there—to enable us to survive in times of deprivation. Your body holds on to stores of food it otherwise would have expended, keeping them around your middle, to draw from when needed. That explains the little ring around the tummy that some of us have trouble getting rid of.

Again, frequent infections and inflammation are other symptoms that may develop, sometimes over the course of many years. Inflammation related to arthritis can be exacerbated by IBS, allergies, and other factors, and it will go unchecked if our adrenal glands are not producing the anti-inflammatory hormones we need.

Depression can come as a result of the failure of epinephrine, a neurotransmitter, to do its job and produce positive feelings. Some people become so desperate for an adrenaline rush that they go bungee-jumping and seek other types of thrills that produce good feelings in the brain. It is possible to wear out your receptors to the point where they simply ignore the adrenaline. This also happens when we overdo our intake of caffeine and other stimulants, always reaching for them to get us through the day.

Here are two additional conditions that chronic stress can lead to.

HYPERLIPIDEMIA

This is the technical term for high cholesterol—the presence of excess fats (lipids) in the blood. It can contribute to high blood pressure because one of the chemicals secreted by the adrenal glands is aldosterol, which elevates blood pressure.

INSULIN RESISTANCE/DIABETES

This condition can occur due to a rapid rise in blood sugar as part of a reaction to a stressor, such as a stressful environment. Our adrenal glands are thinking, "She's going to need energy to get through this, so let's secrete hormones to raise her blood sugar; she is always stressed out, which leads to low blood sugar." We then reach for something salty or sugary to quickly raise our blood sugar, but then we often forget to eat another meal—it's like a blood-sugar seesaw. All of us have been there at one time or another. I know I have. And too much of this cycle can lead to insulin resistance, which can lead to diabetes.

Then, you have people who simply say, "I just don't feel good." They can't quite put their finger on what's bothering them. If you don't feel good in general—if you feel that the zest of life is lacking—it could be that your adrenal glands are shot.

Phase 3: Burnout

In the final phase—burnout—your adrenal glands finally say, "That's it; we can't do it." During the alarm phase and resistance phase, they've enlarged, or hypertrophied, and the cells have grown to try to keep up with the demands being placed on the organs. The adrenal glands reach a point where they can grow no larger, and they begin to shrivel from overuse and abuse. The symptoms associated with this phase relate to premature aging. People look older than they should, such as someone who has been through a terrible grief and looks pale, sallow, and grey in complexion. If these visible qualities persist, it may be that this person is in the burnout phase. It is possible to skip phases one and two and to find oneself in phase three because of having used up one's adrenal reserves in a stressful experience. That's a double whammy.

A difficult experience decreases our resistance to stress, and so everything becomes stressful—intolerably so—and we are subject to chronic fatigue, fibromyalgia, and other ailments. The adrenal glands produce all these chemicals that cause us to burn energy. With that burning of energy comes a series of by-products, including water, a waste product we eliminate through the digestive tract. If you have inflammation in the digestive tract, it is possible to produce by-products at a faster rate than your body can dispose of them, and they will start to build up in your muscles. Thus, you feel knots and experience chemical sensitivity.

The smallest of triggers can produce an extreme reaction. You may smell perfume from fifty feet away and feel yourself getting a headache, but the perfume isn't to blame; it's your anxiety and lack of motivation.

Lack of motivation is a big one. I know a lot of us have big hopes and dreams and feel called to do great things. But if your adrenal glands are dysfunctional, you'll lack the motivation necessary to fulfill your potential. So, for that reason alone, it is really important to nurture these organs.

A patient came to me suffering from IBS, multiple food allergies, insomnia, and weight gain. I administered a salivary test to assess her adrenal glands. In my estimation, she was in between the resistance and burnout phases. Every morning, she had just enough energy to get up and go to work. She deals with family court and has witnessed heartbreak after heartbreak—for ten years—as families are torn apart, often due to her own decision that a parent is not fit to take care of the children, who must then be removed from the home. She'd had a difficult pregnancy and had never completely regained her health. She'd managed to adapt to the stress of her job until her high-risk pregnancy, which propelled her into the burnout phase and left her there. So, I said, "Okay, let's check your adrenal glands." In the morning, she had an okay reading. At noon, it was below normal, just as it was in the evening. She said that she cannot make it through the day unless she consumes a 16-ounce Coke at noon. I told her, "I can't imagine why." Her one saving grace is that she does not have trouble sleeping at night. In fact, she often wants to go to bed as early as 7 o'clock, which makes sense, based on her cortisol pattern. She has a difficult time waking up, but she can do it.

Another indicator of burnout is if you experience dizziness when you stand up, or if your energy dips late in the afternoon. Do you find yourself at a coffee shop every day around three o'clock for a 20- or 30-ounce boost of caffeine? Do you tend to get a "second wind" after 6 o'clock? Do you need more rest than seems necessary? (For example, do you still feel tired after sleeping nine hours?) If you answered yes to any of these questions, it's a clue that your adrenal glands might not be functioning optimally. Are you always complaining that you're cold? It's your thyroid trying to take over. Do you have allergies or rashes that have gotten worse? Gum disease or tooth decay? All of these conditions may be symptomatic of poor adrenal function. Lastly, how is your libido? Does it seem low or nonexistent? I cannot tell you how many women suffer from a decreased libido and don't know that it's treatable.

COMBATING ADRENAL FATIGUE

First, you should evaluate your diet, especially in terms of your intake of salt and sugar. If you add salt to your food, try to use sea salt or Himalayan crystal salt, which is not bleached or tainted after it's harvested. The darker the salt's color, the better it is, because nothing in nature is naturally as white as most salt crystals you see on the shelves.

> *It's important to supplement your natural intake of vitamins and minerals. Even if you're getting your recommended daily allowance, you aren't getting enough.*

It's also important to supplement your natural intake of vitamins and minerals. Even if you're getting your recommended daily allowance, you aren't getting enough. RDAs are set by the government, and they're intentionally low to prevent overdosing.

It is crucial for you to eat whole foods—foods that have not been chemically or mechanically altered. Think chicken breasts instead of chicken nuggets. Select complex sugars over simple sugars. Opt for complex carbohydrates—brown rice over instant white rice, whole-wheat bread over white bread. In brown rice, the fiber is still encapsulated; it hasn't been bleached or mechanically removed.

Complex carbohydrates, when consumed with protein, prevent rapid spikes in your blood sugar and keep your adrenal glands from being stressed. The best way to keep your blood sugar stable throughout the day is to incorporate protein into every meal, as well as a healthy fat source, such as olive oil, flaxseed oil, or fish oil.

Breakfast is a crucial meal. Consume a "complex" variety, such as a whole-grain English muffin and an egg, which incorporates protein, carbohydrates, and fat. You may choose to eat small meals throughout the day—grazing, as it's commonly called. It can help keep your blood sugar level stable.

Avoid excessive stimulants. I am not saying that you can't have your coffee in the morning, but a little bit ought to do it. There have been studies linking it to the prevention of Alzheimer's disease because of how coffee increases blood flow to the brain. And many people find that a little coffee improves their ability to focus. The key word here is *little*. Those who refill their mugs three or four times a day—caffeine addicts—are doing themselves more harm than good.

Now to the tough part. You have to do your homework. A wise medicine man once told me, "There is no pill that you can take to substitute for a poor lifestyle."

Many patients come in and tell me, "Oh, I am very, very healthy. I take twenty-three supplements every day; I drink three glasses of green tea a day; I eat plenty of salmon." Then, when I ask how many hours of sleep they're getting each night, they'll say, "Oh, three or so." Sleep is vital! It allows our bodies to repair themselves; it calms the mind and, in effect, sets everything back to homeostasis. It is very, very important. Try to get at least seven hours—that's what statistics have shown to be the minimum amount to constitute a good night's sleep. Also, if you are waking to use the bathroom at night, try to avoid water after dinner. Drink your recommended six to eight glasses of water throughout the day and try to cut if off by 7:00 p.m. That way, you are not up all night urinating. If you still find yourself up all night urinating, I encourage you to talk to your doctor, because there are a lot of options for dealing with that.

Exercise can contribute to better sleep, and it doesn't have to be intense—walking is a great activity, and it requires no special equipment, aside from a good pair of shoes and an open road (or a treadmill). Stretching is another good way. If you don't feel well enough to actually get up and go, at least perform some stretches. Cycling is another option if low-impact exercise is your priority. You can prevent the wear and tear to your knees caused by walking and running. Particularly if you are postmenopausal, I encourage you to incorporate some form of resistance training, because our bones need all of the help they can get at that point.

If you feel like you are dealing with a significant amount of stress, you need to decrease your output—the energy and time you are expending.

The last thing, which is probably the most difficult "exercise" to do, is just saying no. We tend to fill our calendars to the max with many unnecessary things. If you feel like you are dealing with a significant amount of stress, you need to decrease your output—the energy and time you are expending. Reevaluate your priorities and eliminate, at least for a time, any activities that are not absolutely indispensable.

You would be surprised how much even the most minor of activities can zap your energy. For example, if you are worrying about what is going to happen on a certain television show, your mind may interpret your suspense as legitimate stress. One tendency I've had to work on is my "need" to know what is going on in the world. It is possible to watch too much world news. Of course, it's important to know what is going on, especially so that we can pray for various situations. But we should avoid getting too wrapped up in it, because it may prove detrimental to our health. Our aim should be to care about each situation, pray about it, and release it to God.

•••

I hope that this teaching from my daughter has helped you to better understand the effects of stress on our bodies. If you would like to learn more about Spice and her practice, you may visit www.inspiremedicine.com.

CHAPTER 4

Erase the Pain of Your Past

I want to share an incredible revelation God has blessed me with: You can erase the pain of your past. It's true. Don't believe me? Let me tell you about some of the things I have experienced—and some things God has done—that prove it *is* possible. This revelation has the power to transform your life and to alter the course of your future.

Too many people allow their pasts to keep them from enjoying the future. And, for years, I was among them! I used to say, "I can't do that." I didn't believe in myself because of the verbal abuse I suffered as a child (not from my parents). Repeatedly, I was called "dumb," "stupid," and "ignorant"; I was told, "You'll never amount to anything"; I was told that I was "retarded." God only knows what I would have been capable of, had I not internalized all of these negative remarks. They prevented me from performing well in school and also kept me from finishing college.

Yet those words no longer have an effect on me. How else could I have authored numerous books, created multiple teaching series, and established a powerful ministry that takes me all over the world? I am neither stupid nor retarded, but I needed to break loose from the pain of my past in order to reach the place where I am today.

> **God wants to turn your pain into your passion.**

God wants to turn your pain into your passion. The pain that I have endured throughout my life is not my passion; my passion is to see others healed and made whole.

Right now, I want to take you a step further beyond forgiveness. This is the time to literally wipe away all of the pain and traumatic memories of your past. Think of this process as a Holy Ghost "Etch A Sketch" that allows you to take every negative image and obliterate it with a couple of shakes. After you've erased the image, you can't get it back; it is gone forever. This is what God wants to do with all of your negative memories—all of the hurts and pains of your past. He wants to give you a little shake to wipe away the bad. Then, through His Holy Spirit, He will make you a new creation who remembers only good and beautiful things.

GOD'S "BRAG BOOK"

Many mothers like to make "brag books," scrapbooks filled with photos, awards, drawings, and other items pertaining to their children. I worked really hard on a brag book for my firstborn. When my second daughter was born, I didn't put forth as great an effort. By the births of my third and fourth daughters, I had resigned myself to placing their photos and projects in a box for them to use later in making their own brag books. All my brag books have this in common: they don't include anything negative. No bad report cards, no pictures of children just after wetting their pants, no tally of how many minutes they spent in timeout.

Here is a story I definitely would never include: when one of my daughters was about one-and-a-half years old, I went into her bedroom and found her bouncing in her crib, having a great time. I smiled, until I looked beyond her at the wall. It was smeared—artistically, I might add—with whatever surprise my daughter had found in her diaper. Needless to say, I did not take a picture to stick in her scrapbook.

Instead, I included pictures of her learning to walk, report cards showing straight A's, and letters of acceptance and offers of academic scholarships from various colleges and universities.

That's what God puts in His "brag book" about each of us. In God's Book of Life, He records all of the good that we do, not all of the bad we've committed.

No Record of Wrongs

The Bible says that God is love (see 1 John 4:8, 16), and love *"keeps no record of wrongs"* (1 Corinthians 13:5). In fact, God forgets all our wrongs; He says, *"I, even I, am the one who wipes out your transgressions for My own sake; and I will not remember your sins"* (Isaiah 43:25 NASB). And He wants us to forget them, too!

Have you ever seen the movie *Secretariat?* I love that movie, not least of all because the horse had such a big heart. He ran and ran and ran, faster than any other horse, and won the Triple Crown: the Kentucky Derby, the Preakness Stakes, and the Belmont Stakes. I was fascinated by his trainer, Lucien Loren, who saved snippets of articles and photos of his losses. He kept these newspaper clippings in his wallet and carried them everywhere, as a constant reminder of his failures. Whenever he needed to take out some cash, he saw those clippings and thought again about the times when he'd fallen short. Then, when Secretariat started winning, his

> *Even though God has a far better memory than I do, He chooses to forget my sins and doesn't count them against me.*

trainer got rid of all of those papers and threw them in the trash. When he did this, I thought, *Hallelujah!* But most of us are like Lucien Loren. We store up all of our failures. We may not carry reminders of them in our wallets, but we bury them in our hearts.

Let's cast off our disappointments and failures—and let's do it now! Not over the course of six months but today, this very minute. I have a great memory, which I like to think I inherited from my mom. Her memory was phenomenal. And I thank God for giving me a great memory. But I'm even more thankful that, even though God has a far better memory than I do, He chooses to forget my sins and doesn't count them against me.

He chooses to forget our sins—isn't that good news? We have this assurance from Him: *"For I will be merciful to their iniquities, and I will remember their sins no more"* (Hebrews 8:12 NASB). Hallelujah! And here's another: *"Their sins and their lawless deeds I will remember no more"* (Hebrews 10:17 NASB). No more! I just love that one.

King David

I want to talk a little bit about King David, whom God called *"a man after My own heart, who will do all My will"* (Acts 13:22 NKJV). Yet David sinned big-time—he had an affair with a married woman, and then, as if that wasn't bad enough, he had her husband killed to "cover up the evidence," so to speak. How could an adulterer and a murderer be a man after God's heart? What is wrong with this picture? Why would God make him one of the greatest kings who ever lived? Why would He honor David and shower him with favor?

Imagine David's arrival in heaven. He sees God face-to-face for the first time, and he says, "I really can't believe I did what I did. I am so sorry. I can't believe I had an affair with Bathsheba and then had her husband murdered." God opens up the Book of Life and starts flipping through the pages. After a few minutes, He looks up and says, "David, I don't have it recorded in here that you ever did those things. My record says that you were a man after My own heart. I don't even know what you are talking about. All of your sins have been washed as white as snow."

Imagine the wondrous relief David would feel! It will be the same way when we go to heaven. When God opens up the Book of Life, all He will see is a record of what we did to please Him—our sins won't be written there.

What are you going to say to God when you get to heaven? Will you say, "God, I am so sorry I did drugs"? "I am so sorry for the abortion I had"? "I am so sorry that I was a homosexual"? "I am so sorry that I molested those children"? If you have already repented and asked for forgiveness, the entries of those sins have been erased from the Book of Life, because *"if we confess our sins, he is faithful and just and will forgive us our sins and purify us from all unrighteousness"* (1 John 1:9). The blood of Jesus Christ has cleansed you from all unrighteousness. And the result is that your pages in the Book of Life are pure white.

Apostle Paul

Paul wrote,

Not that I have already obtained all this, or have already been made perfect….But one thing I do: Forgetting what is behind and straining

toward what is ahead, I press on toward the goal to win the prize for
which God has called me.... (Philippians 3:12–14)

He was saying, in essence, "I have done some things that I wish I
had not have done. But, in order for me to do what God has called me
to do, I *must* forget those things that are behind me and press on in
pursuit of my calling. If I were to hold on to those things from my past,
God could not use me in the way He wants to."

Paul was encouraging us to forget those things that are behind so
that we can wholeheartedly pursue all that God has called us to do and
to be.

If anyone had reason to doubt his ability to pursue God's call on his
life, it was Paul. Prior to his conversion to Christianity, Paul, formerly
known as Saul, had made it his mission to imprison and murder as many
Christians as he could. And he was highly successful in this pursuit.
Then, he was saved—but how hard would it have been to believe that
his conversion was authentic? Many Christians probably wondered, *Is he
just saying he's saved so he can get close to us and kill us?* Surely, Paul would
have been aware of such suspicions.

For many people, this would have been enough to convince them
to stay out of the ministry. Paul could have thought, *Nobody's going to
trust me, so I'll just sit at home and study the Scriptures for myself. I feel called
to preach the gospel, but who will listen to me?*

But that isn't what he did. Rather, he chose to forget his past—
to cast off his doubts about how he would be received, based on his
former character—and to go out and preach the gospel, as God had
commanded him to do.

How many people allow their pasts—their past experiences, past
attitudes and behaviors, and so forth—to keep them from doing what
God has called them to do?

Don't let the enemy keep you from what God has called you to do.
And don't let you yourself stand in the way, either!

VISION BLOCKERS

To me, there are few sights more beautiful than the ocean. I'm from Florida, and I love to drive around and marvel at the shimmering, crystal-clear waters of the Gulf of Mexico. One time, I was riding around the Tampa area with my daughter Melody. She was driving, and I was enjoying the luxury of looking out the window and admiring the scenery. It was absolutely breathtaking—until, all of a sudden, splat! A seagull had relieved itself right onto the windshield—on my side, of course. Melody exclaimed, "Look at that, Mom!" I said, "I'd love to see it, but it's kind of hard with all of this stuff on the windshield. Why don't you turn on the wipers?"

It was such a mess. Melody triggered the wiper fluid and turned on the wipers, but all they did was spread white chalky stuff all across the windshield. What had started as a small smudge had spread everywhere, making it even harder to see out. Meanwhile, Melody was still saying, "Wow! Would you look at that!" and I was reminding her, "I can't. There's junk in the way."

> *God wants to come in and clean up the mess in our hearts because He wants us to be able to focus on the vision of what He has called us to do.*

Life is like that sometimes. Situations arise, most of them more serious than a splatter of bird droppings on the windshield, and they block our vision. Often, we make matters worse when we try to clean them up. The more we talk about the traumas we have faced, the worse they become, just as the more Melody ran those windshield wipers, the more the mess spread. We were trying to fix the problem without the proper tools, and it took a trip through a car wash to rid the windshield of all traces of the gunk. After that, we could see clearly again, and I resumed marveling at the beautiful beaches we passed.

What we need is a "Holy-Ghost wash." The Bible says that Christ *"loved the church and gave Himself for her, that He might sanctify and cleanse her with the washing of water by the word"* (Ephesians 5:25–26 NKJV). God wants to come in and clean up the mess in our hearts. He won't merely spread it around so that it obstructs our vision, because He wants us to be able to focus on the vision of what He has called us to do.

HEALING MUST BEGIN WITHIN

Many years ago, my mom had an ulcer on her leg. She had bumped the leg while suffering from phlebitis and diabetes, and even after she'd been healed of both of those conditions, she still had a little prick on her skin. She applied some antibiotic ointment and covered the area with a Band-Aid. When she checked it a few days later, she saw that it had gotten bigger, and she started using larger Band-Aids.

This continued for a year; the mark grew continually. When it reached the size of a silver dollar, my mom decided to go to her doctor and have him take a look at it. She did, and her doctor told her to go to the hospital right away. He warned her that a failure to seek immediate treatment could prove fatal.

So, Mom went to the hospital, and the surgeons anesthetized her leg and cleaned out the ulcer, which had gotten infected. The next day, they scraped the area until blood started flowing over the wound once more. They continued doing this for twelve days. The doctors did not want the infection to close up, so they kept cleaning it out and scraping off any dried blood to rid the area of all traces of bacteria.

It healed perfectly. If they had allowed it to heal over, it would have left a hole there, even under the skin.

The emotional "infections" we experience require the same treatment. A physical infection in the heart can prove fatal, and so can an emotional "infection" of the same organ. Think of the infections you've acquired because of the trauma the enemy has inflicted on your life. God wants to come in with a "Holy-Ghost scalpel" and clean out all the infection, clear away all the junk, and let the brilliant-red, healing blood of Jesus flow through you.

BLOCK OUT THE BAD

I understand the pain of divorce because I've experienced it firsthand. In 2000, I was faced with a divorce because my husband had not been faithful in marriage and would not renounce his homosexual lifestyle. I also understand the devastation of being deserted by one's father because mine left long before I was even born.

And I know the bitterness of guilt because I grew up thinking, *If my mom had not gotten pregnant with me, my parents would probably still be together.* My mom raised my brother and me by herself, and she worked extremely hard to support us. Keeping food on the table was never easy, and I can remember going at night to a nearby grocery store— not to shop, mind you, but to go around back to the dumpster. Mom would hoist my brother up and over the side, and he would dig around in the trash for any salvageable produce. We would return home with rotting peaches and other nasty refuse. Believe me, I understand what it means to be poor. It was a good thing we lived in Florida, because we couldn't afford to heat our house. Today, I rejoice that I can go to the grocery store and purchase as many peaches as I want—peaches that are perfectly ripe, without as much as one bruise.

In addition to growing up impoverished, I suffered abuse—as I wrote earlier, my uncle molested me. And if it's possible for me to forget those events, it's possible for you to do the same. I have no visual recollection of the traumas I've mentioned. At the end of this chapter, I am going to pray for all of your bad memories to be wiped away, just as mine were.

I'll give you an example of an area where you would expect me to have negative memories, but where only positive ones prevail. My ex-husband is a brilliant man. He is very gifted and has many talents. We always had fun traveling, whether in the ministry or on vacation; we went to Hawaii, to Acapulco, all over. He was a phenomenal coach as I was birthing our four daughters. He was a good provider, and he did everything in his power to make sure each of our children had an excellent education.

What I'm trying to show is that, even though I was deeply hurt by his decision to pursue his lifestyle, and even though we got a divorce, all I can recall are the positive things. I am aware of his lifestyle, but what have stayed with me are the positive things that he did for our family. The memory of the pain has vanished. It's gone. And I want to reiterate that I have a great memory. I have a phenomenal memory. But I don't remember those things.

As I was writing this book, I had an interesting encounter. I walked into a church to hear a friend of mine speak. When I saw the pastor, I remembered that he had hurt me about three years prior. Yet I couldn't remember what he'd done! We greeted each other as if nothing negative had ever happened between us.

Forgive and Forget

An important aspect of this "memory loss" is the act of forgiveness. As I wrote in my book *Healing the Heart*, the way that we can know that we have truly forgiven someone who has hurt us, betrayed our trust, or deserted us is when the good memories of that person outweigh the bad—when the pain of what he or she did to us goes away. It's rare for this to happen overnight, but God's love has the power to ease and ultimately erase the aches and pains until the hurt becomes just another past experience—something we learn from and never repeat; something that prepares us to be used by God to minister to others.

> *The way that we can know that we have truly forgiven someone who has hurt us, betrayed our trust, or deserted us is when the good memories of that person outweigh the bad.*

Again, when I look back on the twenty-five years my ex-husband and I spent together, I now remember the good times we had together, not the bad. As I said, he is very intelligent and capable, and I always felt he had the answer to everything. He pushed our girls a lot harder than I would have during their school years. He knew the importance of a good education and was determined that our daughters would do as well as they could in school. They have all achieved great things, and I know that their father's encouragement was a positive influence on them.

Someone said to one of my girls, "It must have been hard growing up with your dad."

I love how she responded. She said, "Not really. He made me try harder and do better in school. My parents both made sacrifices to make sure we got a good education. What I remember most is him sitting me on the counter and drying my *looonnnggg* hair for me."

When she told me this, it really touched my heart. A few years prior, I had ministered to her in the area of unforgiveness. I'd had her begin with forgiving me, and then we'd moved on to additional family members and friends.

Once more, when we've truly forgiven someone, we remember only the good. Did my ex-husband deserve to be forgiven? Does any of us? The answer, of course, is no. However, our heavenly Father forgives us daily as we miss the mark and fall. We also have to extend forgiveness whether the other person wants it or not. Unforgiveness doesn't hurt the other person. It hurts us. Bitterness can destroy our bodies. Hate breeds more hate until love is squeezed out of our lives. Fear takes over and isolates us from anyone who could harm us *or* help us. Do you want to be miserable the rest of your life because of an injustice from years ago? The other person has gone on with his or her life and may even have forgotten what happened. Choose God! Choose to forgive, and then forget it![4]

> *Not that I have already attained, or am already perfected; but I press on, that I may lay hold of that for which Christ Jesus has also laid hold of me. Brethren, I do not count myself to have apprehended; but one thing I do,* **forgetting those things** *which are behind and reaching forward to those things which are ahead, I press toward the goal for the prize of the upward call of God in Christ Jesus. Therefore let us, as many as are mature, have this mind; and if in anything you think otherwise, God will reveal even this to you.*
>
> (Philippians 3:12–15 NKJV, emphasis added)

Like the apostle Paul, I forget *"those things which are behind."* With God's help, I have turned my pain into passion—a passion to see others healed in body, mind, soul, finances, and every other area. A passion to help others release the pains of their pasts and forget all of the junk that's happened to them.

---

[4] See Joan Hunter, *Healing the Heart* (New Kensington, PA: Whitaker House, 2007), 110–112.

Here is another testimony of someone forgetting the pain of her past, thanks in large part to my learning how to turn my pain into my passion:

> This weekend, I had the privilege and opportunity to attend the three-day…conference.

> As Joan walked through her healing books, it dawned on me at one point that I no longer had bitter feelings toward my husband *at all.* Every feeling of anger and resentment was gone. When I realized that I could not even recall past hurts, I began to cry. For most of the session, I continued to cry because I didn't realize how bound I was with unforgiveness. FYI: If all the tissue boxes were empty on the left side of the church, it was because of me!

> He and I have been married for almost thirty-seven years. As I sat and tried to remember the hurts, I couldn't! I could not recall past hurts. It's as if that part of my memory has been erased.

> The new and renewed love I now have for my husband is incredible. Before, I had such a struggle with speaking words of encouragement or positive words about him. Do you know that he is a genius? He is an incredibly gifted man, and to think that I could not see for years and years and years (did I mention years?) that he is handsome, strong, gifted, and a wonderful husband.

> As I gave it further thought, I had another epiphany…: so many people are bound up in unforgiveness and hurt. So many people are walking around with unresolved issues in their hearts. But I now have the tools that I can study so that others can be set free!

Choose to Let Go

Recently, in a store at the airport, I saw a magazine with a prominent couple featured on the cover and a headline indicating that the man had had an affair that had resulted in the birth of a child. *I can relate to that, minus the child part,* I thought as I picked up the magazine and started to read. Seconds later, I closed it again and said, "No! I am not opening the door for all of that junk to come back in. I cut off those words, in Jesus' name. I command those feelings to go." If I had read on, I would have opened myself up to the return of the feelings associated with my ex-husband's infidelity and the divorce that followed.

The other people in the store probably thought I was talking on my cell phone, because I kept saying, "No, no, no; you're not coming in and dwelling in me. I refuse to let the enemy come in and torment me with the information in this magazine." With that, I placed the magazine back on the rack.

> *Are you serving the Lord, or are you serving your past?*

I share this story primarily to show the importance of refusing those feelings every time they threaten to return. That is our responsibility.

People tell me about traumatic things that have happened to them, and I say, "When did this occur?" "Thirty-eight years ago." "Thirty-eight years ago? It's time to get rid of it! Let's put it on the altar, get your heart cleansed, erase the pain of your past, and move on."

Joshua 24:15 says, *"Choose for yourselves this day whom you will serve.... But as for me and my household, we will serve the LORD."* Are you serving the Lord, or are you serving your past? If you are holding on to the past—if you dwell on what has been, to an unhealthy degree—then it has become an idol in your life.

Delete the Painful Memories from Your Mind and Body

Memories are not only stored in the mind—conscious and subconscious—they're stored in the physical cells, as well. As we have seen, those who suffer physical trauma often experience lasting aches and additional trauma to the parts of their bodies that were affected, and doctors have noted that trauma is stored primarily in the cellular memory of the lymph nodes.

I have noticed that many people who have been sexually abused have problems when they are intimate with their spouses. Many of them experience pain and other issues, due mostly to the trauma of the affected areas.

When I'm teaching a healing school, I always tell those in attendance that if they have ever experienced sexual abuse to put their hands on the tops of the insides of their legs, where some of their lymph nodes are located, and to curse the spirit of trauma and command the lymph nodes to be free of any and all stress. Many have told me later that it was amazing what it did for their intimate marital relations.

Turn Your Pain into Your Passion

You, too, can turn your pain into your passion. You, too, can minister anywhere in the world, and to anyone—from a single person at the grocery store to thousands of people at a healing crusade. I want you to have the same experiences I have had. I want you to realize how awesome it is to find freedom and then to see others set free.

When you are bound, it's as if you are wrapped in a straightjacket. You really can't do anything. The pain of the past can be a straightjacket that keeps you from blossoming into all that God has called you to be. You can't even worship God. Today, God wants to untie the straightjacket and loosen the chains so that you are freed to worship Him and do everything else He has called you to do and to be all that you were born to be.

It is an awesome feeling to do what you know you were born to do. I know that I am doing what I was born to do. And I say this not out of pride, because I have been to hell and back to get here; I have paid the price for where I am today. My desire is that you would learn from my experience and find the freedom Christ has for you. I want you to be healed and set free!

See Yourself Free

How do you see yourself? What is your self-perception? Do you see yourself as a widow? Do you primarily identify yourself as a divorcé(e)? After my divorce, I felt like I had a massive letter "D" on my chest or around my neck and that nobody wanted to have anything to do with

> *If you have been through an experience that you feel has given you a label, you need to get up and start again.*

me—especially when it came to the church and my ministry. I felt that being divorced had given me a label, a sort of warning sign, that made churches wary of scheduling me to speak. But I didn't let that stop me.

If you have been through an experience that you feel has given you a label, you need to get up and start again. The people who are successful in life are those who get up again and again and again. When the enemy tries to shut you down in any area, you need to get back up again.

NEGATIVE MEMORIES ERASED

One key to getting up again and starting fresh is escaping the negative memories holding you back. The following are some examples of those who have escaped the painful memories of their pasts. Read them and be encouraged—you, too, can cast off every negative memory and embrace a positive future!

An Abusive Past Forgotten

A woman came to me, wanting me to lead her in a prayer for forgiveness for the way she'd treated her sons, who are now grown, when they were young. She told me that she'd often beaten them, and that she'd been forced to go to counseling for years to manage her anger and to avoid having the boys taken away from her. We prayed, but her mind clung to the memory and the guilt. She said, "I just really wish that I hadn't beaten my sons when they were young." I reminded her that we'd already prayed for forgiveness, but she wouldn't let it go. So, I decided to try something for the first time and see if it would work. I prayed, "Father, right now, in the name of Jesus, thank You for wiping out the pain of her past and the memory where her children are concerned."

After that, the woman said, "I'm going to ask my sons to forgive me one more time."

"Okay," I replied.

She went to her sons and said to them, "You know, I have one major regret in my life. And that major regret is that I beat you when you were younger."

"You didn't beat us," her sons replied. "You were disciplining us, and you spanked us."

Then, she went to her husband and said, "I really wish I had not beaten our boys."

He responded, "You were just a strong disciplinarian." Meanwhile, he was the one who had taken his wife to seek counseling so that she'd stop beating their children!

God totally took away the memory of this woman's abusiveness from her husband and sons. Today, one of her sons has children of his own—two little boys—and his mother often babysits them. No longer does she struggle with anger or lash out. Talk about a miracle! God heard her prayer and healed her completely. As a bonus, He also healed her boys.

There is incredible power and freedom in forgiveness, but we're talking about much more than forgiveness. We're talking about getting rid of the thing that needed to be forgiven!

A Daughter's Memory Erased

I have a friend named Susan who became interested in the idea of praying for "memory erasure" and tried it on herself in regard to something she regretted having done to her daughter. When she approached her daughter to talk about the issue and to seek her forgiveness, her daughter said, "Mom, if you want to talk to me, at least talk about something that really happened." In her daughter's mind, it was as if it had never happened at all. As far as she was concerned, her mother had never done what she was confessing to.

Healed Emotionally and Physically from Rape

Another friend of mine was the victim of a gang rape before she was saved. As a result, she became pregnant and gave birth to a son, whom she gave up for adoption. That was more than twenty years ago. Today, God is restoring her relationship with her son.

He has healed her in other ways, as well. When she was raped, her attackers dragged their fingernails across her bare back, causing pain and significant bleeding and leaving a lot of scarring. One day, she was getting out of the shower, and she heard a voice say, "Look at your back."

She instinctively responded, "Get thee behind me, Satan! I don't want to look at my back. It reminds me of everything that happened to me."

"Don't you know My voice?" It was God speaking to her. "Look at your back. Look at your back."

Finally, she turned around and checked the reflection of her back in the bathroom mirror. All of the scars and ribbons of flesh were gone. Her beautiful, smooth back had been restored! Today, she is in a position of leadership at her church, and God is using her to minister with incredible results to many people, especially victims of rape. Just as He did for me, God turned her pain into her passion! And He wants to do the same for you.

Healed from Trauma Endured in Vietnam

This next story happened in 2011 at a healing service. I've already received several praise reports since I prayed for a man there whose helicopter had been blown to bits while he was a soldier in Vietnam. Miraculously, he'd survived the explosion, but he required neck surgery. During the procedure, the surgeons had severed some nerves, and they grew back incorrectly, causing him excruciating pain that no drug could dull.

I put my hands on his shoulders and back and prayed for him, saying, "I curse this spirit of trauma, in Jesus' name. I command all traces of post-traumatic stress disorder to go, in Jesus' name. I speak health and wholeness into this area. I command all pain to go and the nerve endings to grow back together properly, in Jesus' name. I speak height restored because of the vertebrae in his neck and back that were destroyed in the accident." Then, I laid hands on his head and said, "Father, I thank You for erasing the pages of his past. I thank You for erasing all of the pain and the nightmares he has had, night after night, for forty-two years. All of the images of the helicopter going down, I command to go, and I speak sweet sleep."

He started crying, laughing, weeping, and wailing. He was free! His pastor contacted me later to say that he is still doing well, with no more pain, no more nightmares, and no more memories of the helicopter crash. Hallelujah!

Liberated from Guilt

At the same service, I had prayed for another man who had been burdened with guilt ever since four of his friends had died in battle while under his command. I prayed with him and cursed the spirit of trauma, and then I asked God to erase the pain of his past, so that every negative memory related to the deaths of his friends would be gone, and that all he would remember would be the times when they'd laughed and enjoyed one another, even in the midst of war. God honored our prayer, and it was awesome.

Recollection of Childhood Molestation Removed

I know a woman who was molested by her father when she was young. When she got married, making love with her husband was extremely painful, physically, mentally and emotionally. I prayed that God would erase the pain of her past. I also prayed for God to erase the cellular memory of the lymph nodes near the parts of her body affected by the abuse, in the upper parts of her legs. I had her lay her hands there as I cursed the cellular memory and trauma out of those lymph nodes. I also led her in a prayer to forgive her father.

I checked in on her several times over the next several months. She and her husband were enjoying marital relations for the first time after many years of marriage. Today, more than forty years later, instead of seeing an abusive man, she now remembers her dad as a loving father. The pain of her past was gone.

Physical Pain and Mental Anguish Erased

About eight years ago, a woman named Nancy and her husband attended a service. I asked everyone stand up and measure his or her arms. We discovered that one of Nancy's arms was between four and six inches shorter than the other arm—a considerable difference! I asked her to come to the front so that we all could watch as she was healed. She was standing two or three feet away from me when I prayed for everyone's arms to grow. I said, "Father, in the name of Jesus, I command all of these arms to grow." All of a sudden, her arm extended—and the sleeve of her blouse was too short! I exclaimed, "Yeah! Thank You, Jesus!" and everyone started shouting excitedly as they witnessed the same thing I saw.

But God wasn't done with Nancy. Just then—boom! She fell to the ground. Nobody had touched her or pushed her. I hoped she was okay and wondered whether she had been "slain in the Spirit."

I found out later what God had done. Today, she has an incredible testimony. As a young girl, she'd never gone to school sober or straight; she'd always been drunk or high on drugs. She couldn't face life or bear any amount of pain without the help of drugs and alcohol. By the time she turned twelve, she'd had multiple stepfathers. And that number doesn't account for all of the men her mother kept around! Many of those men had abused her, as had her own mother. Whenever she would tell her mom that she was hungry and wanted something to eat, bam! Her mother would hit her—so violently, in fact, that she would bleed and her jaw would be knocked out of joint. She suffered from TMJ as a result.

Even earlier in her life, her biological father had often beaten her, and she had raised her arm in self-defense. Because she had used her arm to protect her face, that arm had borne the brunt of her father's blows. He had beaten her so frequently and so brutally that he had destroyed the growth plate in that arm. When she was around the age of five or six, her arm stopped growing. For most of her adult life, she was institutionalized because she could not function in society. She was a wreck.

Somehow, she got out and got married, but her husband had to readmit her frequently to the institution because she couldn't survive outside. At the institution, she was continually drugged. Her psychiatrist would tell her husband, "Shannon, you need to get yourself a new wife. You're young. Go find a new wife." Shannon would reply, "I don't want a new wife. God gave me Nancy." "There's nothing we can do for her," the doctor would say. "Go on and take her home, but we know she'll be back here again in two weeks." Sure enough, Nancy would go back, just as the doctor predicted. There was nothing he could do beyond giving her drugs.

After a while, Shannon decided that he didn't want Nancy to be drugged up all of the time. He heard that I was coming to town, and so he brought her to my service.

After prayer, she experienced a creative miracle when her arm grew to match the length of her other one. While she was slain in the Spirit, the pain left her arm, her jaw, her hip—everywhere she'd been beaten. It was completely gone.

In the past, whenever she walked, she would say, "Oh, my knee really hurts—that's where 'George' hit me. I remember how horrible that was. Oh, my ankle—it's so weak because of what Sam did to me." Her jaw had been in constant pain from having received so many backhanded hits from her mom, yet God put it back into place and took away all of the pain and inflammation.

Shannon went back to the hospital and said to the doctors, "Thank you for everything you have done. I have a new wife!"

The doctors were excited because they figured he had finally followed their advice and found someone new. Not so! His wife was still the same woman—Nancy, the mother of his children—but she had become a brand-new person because the pain was gone and her distressing memories were healed. She returned to the institution one last time to collect her belongings, and she hasn't been back since. She and her husband are now involved in full-time

> *When God does something, He does it all the way, not just partway.*

ministry. When God does something, He does it all the way, not just partway.

Miraculous Forgiveness

I asked a man to give his testimony one year after I had met him and ministered to him. I told him, "I want you to give your testimony of what God did when I was here last time." He shared that his shoulder had been healed. I said, "Praise God, but I'm talking about your other testimony." I had to remind him of the details. He agreed.

Nineteen years ago, his ex-wife and her boyfriend had murdered his six-year-old daughter. They are still in prison. When I first met this man, he'd said, "If I'd ever seen them, I would have killed them. I would have gladly spent the rest of my life in prison knowing that they were dead." But he forgave them and released them. The result was that all of the pain of the murder and the court case vanished. Not only that, but this man went to the prison to minister to his ex-wife and her accomplice! He prays for them every day and sends them books from time to time. That's freedom! And that's what God wants to give you.

DWELL ON THE GOOD

We read in 3 John 1:2, *"Beloved, I pray that you may prosper in all things and be in health, just as your soul prospers"* (NKJV). God wants us to reach out to Him so that our souls may be nourished and prosper—so that we may enjoy life to the fullest. (See John 10:10.) Jesus says to us, *"Let not your heart be troubled; you believe in God, believe also in Me"* (John 14:1 NKJV). And we have this glorious charge in Philippians 4:8:

> *Finally, brethren, whatever things are true, whatever things are noble, whatever things are just, whatever things are pure, whatever things are lovely, whatever things are of good report, if there is any virtue and if there is anything praiseworthy; meditate on these things.*   (NKJV)

Jesus said, *"The thief does not come except to steal, and to kill, and to destroy. I have come that they may have life, and that they may have it more abundantly"* (John 10:10 NKJV). Are you experiencing the abundant life that God has promised you? I am, and it's awesome. I walk continually in the power and the joy of God, where there is neither oppression nor depression; there's no weakness or wanting to stay in bed all day, every day. I wake up every morning and say, "Hallelujah! It's another day to do awesome work for the kingdom of God. It's another day to bring Him glory and to manifest His miracles in every realm of life—physical, mental, emotional, spiritual, and financial."

We alone have the power to decide what your mind meditate on. It's time to stop dwelling on the pain of your past—it's time to get free! Today is the day to start concentrating on those things that are lovely, true, pure, and of good report. God wants to present you without fault or wrinkle—spotless and blameless. (See also Ephesians 5:27 NKJV, KJV, NIV, NASB.) He does not want your healing to be delayed any longer. He wants you healed and whole. Jude 1:24 says, *"Now to him who is able to keep you from stumbling, and to present you faultless before the presence of His glory with exceeding joy"* (NKJV).

The waiting is over and done with. Today is the day for your healing! Today is the day for God to erase the pain of your past! Today is the day for you to release all of the traumatic experiences you have endured!

Revelation 10:5–6 says,

The angel whom I saw standing on the sea and on the land raised up his hand to heaven and swore by Him who lives forever and ever, who created heaven and the things that are in it, the earth and the things that are in it, and the sea and the things that are in it, that there should be delay no longer. (NKJV)

Likewise, there shall be no more delay for you! God wants you to have His joy. He wants you to enjoy abundant life. He wants you to be free—completely free in every area. Jesus prayed to His heavenly Father, *"But now I come to You, and these things I speak in the world, that they may have My joy fulfilled in themselves"* (John 17:13 NKJV). He wants His joy to be fulfilled in you. He wants to point to you as an example of His wealth of favor and kindness in all He has done for you through Christ. (See Ephesians 2:7.)

Proverbs 10:7 says that *"the memory of the righteous is blessed"* (NKJV, NASB). Even though this verse refers to remembering the righteous, I think we can apply it to our memories, too. Our memories are not to be full of junk. They aren't to be filled with images from all of the terrible experiences of the past. God wants each of us to have a memory that's blessed. He wants us to be able to reflect on the past and say, for example, "I really did have a good dad," or "I really did have a good ex-husband."

EXPERIENCING FREEDOM

There is a stipulation, however: you need to be willing to accept freedom from your past and to submit to the change it will work in your life. Most people don't like to change, but change is the only way by which the homely worm can transform into a dazzling butterfly. You can't afford to remain in a cocoon of denial about the negative things that happened in the past. Now is the time for your healing to reach completion. It's time to come out of the cocoon, spread your wings, and soar freely like beautiful butterflies.

Consider the following testimony of a woman who underwent a radical transformation from a "worm" mentality to a "butterfly" mind-set.

When I was nineteen years old, I had an unexpected pregnancy and, totally against my own values, had an abortion. I never wanted to have an abortion. From a very young age, I had dreamed of and imagined having ten children. It was a situation where I was uninformed about my options, was without the support of the father (and crushed by his suggestion to have an abortion), and was afraid of disgracing my parents. Confused, alone, and afraid, I did the very last thing I ever wanted to do.

I flew to New York City by myself to have the abortion. (That was the way it was done in the early 70s.) I repented before I even went through with it, and I repented repeatedly—a lot— from that time on. In my heart, I knew God forgave me, but in my mind, I could not imagine how this could ever be forgiven. I was unable to receive His forgiveness and suffered greatly for thirty years.

Whenever I would date someone during my single years, I made sure he knew about the abortion, expecting each one to change his mind about me after that.

For about the first twelve years following my abortion, every time I saw a child who was near the age that my child would have been at the time, I would cry, more so if I was by myself. The pain accelerated when I got pregnant ten years later with my oldest daughter. As I read the books about pregnancy and saw the pictures in the books of the development stages of a baby even as early on as eight or twelve weeks, I was devastated. After my daughter was born, I suffered from postpartum depression for about six weeks, which I felt was related [to my guilt over the abortion].

During the next fifteen years or so, and even after my second daughter was born, I experienced times when I would hear children crying and there were actually no children around, or I would hear children crying and they would be laughing and playing, not crying. It was awful torment. I couldn't think or talk about my abortion without crying, even after thirty years had passed. I still felt unworthy of forgiveness of my sin of having an abortion, and I hated what I had done and blamed myself as a result. I would occasionally go from brushing my hair in the mirror to hitting myself on my head with the brush, purposely causing pain to myself.

Then, one day, I went to a counselor for help and prayer. As we talked, every question he asked brought us to the subject of the abortion. When he prayed for me, he commanded some spirits to go from me, the spirits of guilt and shame being the ones I remember the most clearly. As he prayed, I felt the sensation of what I would describe as a rolling pin rolling up my back, from my waist to my shoulders, and then it rolled off my shoulders. I didn't really understand what had happened at that moment, as I understand now, but I did know one thing: from the time the spirits of guilt and shame left me that day, my life has been completely different.

From that moment on, I no longer cried whenever I thought or talked about the abortion, and it has become a testimony instead—a testimony about how one touch from the delivering, healing power of God changed my life and set me free immediately! I cannot even muster up any guilt or shame about it, even though I know abortion is an awful thing, because God's love and forgiveness have overpowered it! I was finally able to receive God's love and forgiveness for me, and that felt so good. I am able to boldly share my testimony with others who are contemplating abortion or who have already had an abortion, and I allow God to use my experience to help other women.

> *I understand so clearly now that the enemy was trying to keep me from receiving and acknowledging God's love and forgiveness that were mine because of the work of Jesus on the cross.*

The good thing is, I have a son named Daniel in heaven whom I will see one day, and that brings me great joy! [It is important to name your children who are in heaven, whether as a result of abortion, miscarriage, or something else.]

I understand so clearly now that the enemy was trying to keep me from receiving and acknowledging God's love and forgiveness that were mine because of the work of Jesus on the cross. The devil's lies had convinced me—for thirty long years—that I was unworthy of the forgiveness Jesus provided. I am so grateful that God has set me free. I truly don't know where I would be or what I would be doing right now if I had not been set free, but I am pretty sure I would not be living the victorious life that I am now. I give God all the praise and all the glory!

—*Lovely lady today because of Him*

Prayer for Freedom

I would like to pray for you right now, first and foremost, to curse the spirit of trauma in the name of Jesus. Hundreds of people have been healed as a result of this prayer, and I give all the glory to God for this revelation.

To receive this prayer, start by placing your hand over your heart, because we are going to pray for your heart first, followed by other areas of your body that may have been scarred by trauma.

"Father, right now, in the name of Jesus, I send the word of healing through this teaching. Father, I thank You for Your anointing that permeates the person who is reading this right now. In the name of Jesus, I curse the spirit of trauma. I command it to be loosened and to be gone, in Jesus' name. I also curse the spirits of rejection, abandonment, betrayal, abuse, divorce, abortion, grief, feelings of unworthiness, and all related circumstances. I curse every form of heaviness and regret from former lifestyles and past sins. And, Father, right now, in the name of Jesus, I command any trauma relating to rape, molestation, and abortion to go."

If you have been sexually abused, place your hands on the lower part of your body, specifically on your upper thighs where some of your lymph nodes are located, as I pray for you:

"Father, right now, in the name of Jesus, I curse any cellular memory regarding any form of sexual abuse, rape, or sexual trauma. I command the memory to go from the mind, as well as from the cells, in Jesus' name."

If you have ever been hit or physically abused, no matter where on your body, receive this prayer:

"I command the cellular memory of the trauma and the pain to go, in Jesus' name."

Now, I want you to place your hand to your forehead and pray:

"Father, right now, in the name of Jesus, I speak to erase all the pain and the negative memories from my past."

Next, I want you to repeat the following:

First of all, say, "Thank You, Jesus." Second of all, I want to remind you that you have to choose to release it. Just say, "Father, I forgive those who have hurt me. I release them of what they did to me. I know that what they did to me will always be wrong, but I choose to release them and to forgive them for what they did to me. And, Father, I release and forgive anybody who has hurt me physically, sexually, or verbally. I choose this day to release the pain. I don't want to carry it anymore. I don't want to carry the guilt that goes along with it. Father God, I thank You for totally taking all of the guilt, pain, and regret away."

Then, pray this:

"I choose to release this. Thank You, Father, for releasing the pain of my past. Thank You for totally wiping out all of the negative impressions and bad experiences and for leaving only happy memories. *'Create in me a clean heart, O God; and renew a right spirit within me'* (Psalm 51:10 KJV). I want to be a man/woman after Your own heart, as David was."

Now, I want you declare, as loudly as you can, "I am free!" Hallelujah.

Scriptures to Take to Heart

You would forget your misery, and remember it as waters that have passed away. (Job 11:16 NKJV)

He reached down from on high and took hold of me; he drew me out of deep waters. He rescued me from my powerful enemy, from my foes, who were too strong for me. They confronted me in the day of my disaster, but the LORD was my support. He brought me out into a spacious place; he rescued me because he delighted in me. (Psalm 18:16–19)

But one thing I do: Forgetting what is behind and straining toward what is ahead, I press on toward the goal to win the prize for which God has called me heavenward in Christ Jesus. (Philippians 3:13–14)

CHAPTER 5

Walking in Deliverance

I know a young woman who was a victim of satanic ritual abuse (SRA) for twenty-five years. The trauma she suffered—often at the hands of her own parents—was unimaginable. Less imaginable still is the fact that, today, she works in ministry, bringing deliverance to dozens as she travels. Many people can't even conceive of how someone who suffered so much could find freedom, and yet she did, through the power of God. Her name is Michayila Joy Kairos, and she's written a book about her experiences called *Fragments to Freedom*.

MIRACULOUS PHYSICAL HEALING

The first type of deliverance Michayila experienced was physical—the cellular memory from the SRA she suffered was completely erased and the damage reversed. But don't take my word for it. Here is her testimony, as she related it to me:

I wrote out a list of questions for the doctor this morning concerning the rest of what I knew I needed to tell her and ask her about. It's the first time I have ever done that—asked a doctor anything related to my health. Usually, I just listen to her questions and keep my answers as short as possible; I have always tried to get out of the doctor's office as fast as possible. Today was different. This morning, the Wonderful Counselor and I met again, and this is what happened:

I told Him I knew He would be with me, but I was so afraid about asking her what I needed to, and so afraid to hear that my body would have rips and tears that I didn't want her to see, and so afraid that there would be scarring from previous trauma.

I immediately heard Him clearly say, "I am restoring you completely and healing you so completely, it will be as though it is a baby's body, brand-new, completely made new, with no signs of any scarring or trauma, absolutely new and healed. Where there was complete damage in your womb, there will be a completely new womb from Me; where there was scarring and signs of trauma, I am supernaturally making you brand-new. I am bringing healing to your womb completely; it will be as though it is absolutely brand-new, as though you have never carried, with no signs of any trauma. I am restoring you completely. I will make a way, because of My healing, for you to carry and deliver a brand-new baby again who will be totally safe with you. Where there was complete damage in your womb, there will be a completely new womb from Me; where there was scarring and signs of trauma, I am supernaturally making you brand-new." I could hardly believe what He was saying, and I began to weep. I don't often share this, but one of my deepest desires was to have another baby. I had been to few doctors—they never examined me because I wouldn't let them, but they did a test to discover that my cervix would never expand again because of the traumas they discovered, and they told me I would never be able to carry another baby. This was yet another time when I began to hate everyone for all I was made to do. So, I had known for years the reality that I would probably never be able to carry another baby unless the Lord did a miracle in my body…and in my heart.

So, I met with Him, and He asked me to do something I have never done before. He said to me, "As part of My healing work in you, would you be willing to do something that may be very hard?" I asked Him, "What, Lord?" He then asked me to go from the top of my head to the bottom of my feet and process with Him regarding every single area of my body, thanking Him for the way He originally created each part of my body, asking Him to heal anything that needed to be healed in each specific area of my body, and asking Him if there were any memories associated with each part of my body that I had not yet processed with Him, and, if any memories were exposed, to ask the Lord to come and reveal truth to cancel the lies that I had begun to believe with that trauma and memory, asking the Lord if there was any sin I needed to repent of that I hadn't yet regarding that area of my body (and repenting if anything was exposed), and asking the Lord to show me how He saw that area of my body— asking the Lord to supernaturally heal me from all shame and guilt relating to that part of my body.

And then, He would ask me, in regard to each part of my body, "Are you willing to embrace this area of your body, now washed and cleansed, as part of yourself and receive it as part of who I created you to be, part of your wholeness?" He had me repent of every way I had rejected any part of my body as being a part of me and not caring for it. Then, for each part, the Lord would so gently minister to me His comfort as each of these questions was being processed.

My body remembered things my mind never had as I went through this process with the Lord. Many memories I had never processed with Him came up during this time, and I knew He was healing me in those areas. The areas where this took the most time were my private areas, obviously, but with every area, the Lord brought healing and ministered to every place. I knew something was occurring in my womb when I cried out to Him regarding it and asked Him questions. I told Him I'd always wanted to just get rid of my womb—I had rejected it and hated it because of all the pain associated with it. And He so tenderly said, "I am making it as though none of it ever happened. My healing in you is so deep, it will be as though it will be brand-new." He said, "Baby girl, if you want another baby, it would be My delight for you to carry a dream of Mine…. My heart would long for you to carry them and love them, and deliver them, and raise them as their mother. Is that something

> *As I went through this process with the Lord, He brought healing and ministered to every place.*

you would like to do one day?" "Yes, Lord," I said, "the deepest parts of my heart want the chance this time to be a mom."

I knew He was doing a deep work in my body and in my heart but didn't know the extent yet. Other areas that took a while to process through as He was leading were my brain/head, my ears, my eyes, and my mouth, as more memories were remembered when I addressed those areas specifically, as well as my feet (I hadn't really yet processed with the Lord about memories related to my feet and what I was forced to walk through or on, or stand in, or be tied down to, etc., until He also had me process with Him about my feet, the last part of the body I addressed this morning with Him).

I was in the doctor's office when she asked how I was doing. I told her I had some questions for her and had her read them relating to my previous sexual abuse. She explained that, yes, each one of those things needed to be addressed medically, and she was so, so, so sorry that I'd ever had to go through abuse of any kind, especially sexual abuse, as it does so much to a person that is so hard to heal from, emotionally and mentally.

She asked me if it was okay for her to do a complete female exam, including a Pap smear and a breast examination, to check everything that needed to be checked. She also said she didn't want to schedule one until I told her I was ready, but that the sooner I had one, the better. She asked me if I knew what all would take place during the exam, and I told her, honestly, I didn't. So, she explained the whole thing—what they would be checking for and, in my case, what damage would still be affecting anything, to determine whether disease or infection were legitimate concerns. I asked her how long it took, as I really didn't want to have the anxiety about it anymore and fear that something was wrong. I wanted to get it over with. She said it just took a couple of minutes and that we could have results in a couple weeks, when I came back to check up on the other stuff we have been working with. She asked me, "Are you ready to go ahead with it today? I have some time, if you are ready, but it's totally up to you. Otherwise, we can reschedule whenever you are ready."

I wanted healing—complete healing—so I decided I was ready that day, and I told her. She explained what I needed to do and said that she would be back in a few minutes, when I was ready. She left, and when she came back a few minutes later, she asked me how I was doing. She said she would talk me through it the whole way, and that if, at any time, I wanted her to stop, she absolutely would. She gave me a few instructions to make it easier, and then the exam took place. She could tell I was in pain for some of it and said she was so sorry that I had to go through any of that pain and that she would be as gentle as she could. She also used the smallest tools available.

Then, as she was looking and examining, I heard words I didn't believe I would ever hear, and I began to cry right then and there. She said, "Sweetheart, I don't see any signs of tearing or trauma, or any kind of damage that was done to you. It is literally as though you have been made brand-new down here, and it looks perfect, as though you got a whole new body in these parts." Everything had been completely restored by Him, and I began to cry, because that

> *I was overwhelmed by His love to completely cleanse me and make me as though I was literally brand-new, inside and out.*

was exactly what the Wonderful Counselor had told me that morning that He would do. To hear those exact words come out of her mouth right then was the best news I had heard in years! It was literally as though nothing had ever happened—no scars, no damage, no signs of trauma of any kind. I couldn't believe it! My Father had literally healed me there to such an extent as to make it totally brand-new in Him. Then, it was done!

The doctor told me how proud she was of me and said that she thought I was so brave for really wanting to be well again and to have total healing.

I got in my car and wept because of the incredible healing I knew that my Papa had done for me in an area I'd believed would be scarred and destroyed forever. For the first time, I began to dream of another baby girl or baby boy that would be safe in my brand-new womb and that I would be able to carry perfectly fine. I was overwhelmed by His mercy to totally heal me in such a deep area of my heart, if not the deepest. I was so overwhelmed by His love to completely cleanse me and make me as though I was literally brand-new, inside and out. He had restored my virginity. When I met Joan for the first time, she ministered to me about forgiveness, and I got free. She also prayed for my purity to be restored.

Hallelujah! Michayila's doctor confirmed that, in addition to the absence of scarring, she had a new hymen that showed no signs of ever having been torn.

Miraculous Mental Healing

The next area in which Michayila experienced healing was in her mind. God has the power to erase our negative memories so that all that remains are positive, happy thoughts. There is a caveat, however, in that He will allow us to remember just enough so that we'll be equipped to avoid being victimized in the same way. For example, I divorced my husband because he was—and is, at the time of writing this book—living a homosexual lifestyle. Today, I have nothing but positive memories of our marriage, but that doesn't mean that I'm going to get back together with him. God enables me to remember just that much for my own protection.

Read what God did in Michayila's life in regard to her memories of her parents and other abusers:

The Lord has not only healed me to enable me to forgive those who abused me in SRA—those in my family, etc.—but I was asking the Lord awhile ago to remove the memories of the rituals and all that had happened that was horrific. I didn't want them in my mind or the cellular memory in my body anymore. I had heard Joan's teaching on this and wanted it so bad. He did it! He has completely wiped away all the torture, all the memories of the rituals and the horror, that had gone on for over twenty-five years. It really seems unbelievable to me at times because it is like I am "remembering" someone else's life when I just had the knowledge of what goes on because of what I learned growing up (and knew that I experienced repeatedly, but honestly had no memory of it happening to me anymore). I cry just thinking about the goodness of Him to do this inside of me.

Now, instead of remembering all the horror, I remember my dad plowing snow in our backyard to make a skating rink in our backyard for me. I remember my dad teaching me how to play tennis and when he built the slabs for a basketball court and when he bought me a basketball that was bigger than both my hands around it. I remember my dad flying me in his plane and when we would soar in Alaskan skies and have a view like none other in the middle of the Northern Lights. I remember my mom teaching me how to make quilts; I remember my mom making dresses for me, regardless of what might have happened with them later.

And now He is making new memories for me entirely— ones that are good and ones that I can keep forever! Ones that are completely filled with joy, and a life that I never even could dream of living, but that He has brought me into, real abundant life. I so love life now. He has completely transformed my memory and filled it with memories of hope, joy, freedom, and the life that He promised when He came to set me free. He has totally erased the pain of my past and filled those places with more and more passion for Him and a passion to minister that freedom, healing, and life to others. And I'm enjoying being used by Him.

RECOVERING FROM SEXUAL ABUSE AND THE RESULTING COVENANTS

Today, Michayila is all smiles and laughs. By the power of God, she has been freed to talk about her experiences with those who are suffering or who have suffered from SRA and other forms of sexual abuse, and she is blossoming into the person God has called her to be. She is the perfect example of someone who has turned her pain into her passion.

A key to escaping the pain of sexual abuse is to break the covenants that were formed between the abused and the abuser. Sexual acts, consensual or not, constitute a covenant that must be cursed and broken in order for the victim to walk in complete healing.

The Origin and Purpose of Covenants

A covenant is meant to be a good, godly tie between two people. God established His covenant with us—a bond that obliges Him to keep His Word and, in turn, asks that we obey (which is possible only by the perfect sacrifice of Jesus on the cross, on which He shed His blood and by which our sins and shortcomings are forgiven, and by the indwelling Holy Spirit). In the Old Testament, believers made restitution for their sins through animal sacrifices, which was part of their blood covenant with God and a forerunner of Jesus' later sacrifice.

Another blood covenant is marriage—specifically, the sexual union between a man and a woman. It is a holy covenant, about which the Word of God says, *"Let marriage be held in honor among all, and let the marriage bed be undefiled; for fornicators and adulterers God will judge"* (Hebrews 13:4 NASB).

As I wrote in my book *Power to Heal,*

When a man and a woman come together after marriage in the act of intimacy, they are making a holy covenant with each other. There is a shedding of blood when the hymen is broken. Any sexual relations outside of marriage are considered an unholy or ungodly covenant.[5]

Through a sexual covenant, there is a physical and spiritual bond that connects the two individuals. All that they are and everything that they have belongs to one another, for *"they are no longer two but one flesh"* (Matthew 19:6 NKJV). Actually, a covenant is more than merely physical

---

[5]Joan Hunter, *Power to Heal* (New Kensington, PA: Whitaker House, 2009), 76.

and spiritual—it can also be mental or emotional, or a combination of any of these.

Renouncing Ungodly Covenants

Sexual intercourse establishes a covenant that is holy only if it occurs in the context of marriage; all other sexual relations, including those between an abuser and his victim, constitute an unholy covenant that must be broken if the victim is to experience complete healing and wholeness.

Even after my divorce with my ex-husband had been finalized, I was still in covenant with him and with what he was doing. In order to separate myself from him and his sin, I had to renounce the covenant we had made more than two decades earlier.

If you have suffered sexual abuse, if you have gone through a divorce due to your spouse's infidelity but still experience pain in connection with the relationship, and if your circumstances are such that sexual relations are causing you trouble, renounce that covenant in Jesus' name. Use this prayer template to guide you:

"Father, I entered into an ungodly covenant with _____ (insert name). In Jesus' name, I renounce that covenant, and I ask You to take away anything negative that came into my life as a result of it. Thank You, Jesus, that I am set free from that ungodly covenant. Amen."

Forgiving an Abuser

Again, extending forgiveness is a key to healing. If you renounce an ungodly covenant formed through molestation or rape, you still need to offer a prayer of forgiveness for the perpetrator, or that person will hold harmful influence over you and your physical, emotional, mental, and spiritual well-being. As you do so, it is important to use the name of the person—the name by which you refer to him or her.

I met a woman who had been raped who had renounced the ungodly covenant that bound her to her attacker, but her freedom was partial. So, she prayed to forgive him—still to no avail. The Lord showed me in my spirit that she had a different name for the man who had raped her. Even though it was not his given name, it was the name by which she knew him. (I won't share it here, but it was not a nice word.) I told her what the Lord had shown me, and she was amazed. Sure enough, when she prayed and forgave him, saying, "I forgive '—,'" her healing was complete, and she was set free—totally free.

Scriptures to Take to Heart

If you hold to my teaching, you are really my disciples. Then you will know the truth, and the truth will set you free. (John 8:31–32)

If you forgive men when they sin against you, your heavenly Father will also forgive you. (Matthew 6:14)

Praise be to the God and Father of our Lord Jesus Christ, the Father of compassion and the God of all comfort, who comforts us in all our troubles, so that we can comfort those in any trouble with the comfort we ourselves have received from God. (2 Corinthians 1:3–4)

CHAPTER 6

Don't Look Back

We read in Proverbs 26:11, *"As a dog returns to its vomit, so a fool repeats his folly."* Deliverance is not necessarily a one-time event, especially if those who have escaped from trauma and abuse go running back to it again and again. This occurs particularly among women who have been abused physically, verbally, sexually, or emotionally by their husbands or partners, and people often wonder why they return to them—or stay with them. It's a deep-seated psychological issue called *codependency*, and I know the legitimacy of this condition because I was codependent myself.

Merriam-Webster's 11th Collegiate Dictionary defines *codependency* as "a psychological condition or a relationship in which a person is controlled or manipulated by another who is affected with a pathological condition (as an addiction to alcohol or heroin); dependence on the needs of or control by another." To put it simply, someone who is codependent relies on the presence and behavior of another person to control his or her life. And it isn't a healthy way to live.

For twenty-five years, I was codependent on my ex-husband. As I shared in my book *Healing the Heart,*

> I couldn't make any decisions for myself. I tried to do only what was pleasing to my husband. He made all the decisions for the entire family. My opinion was not important or worthwhile. He presided, provided, and decided. I obeyed and fit into his picture of the perfect family. I was afraid to disagree because he wouldn't like me or want me. He might verbally put me down or,

worse yet, abandon me like my birth father had so many years ago.

For many years, I had depended on my mother for approval and love. No one else thought I was worthwhile. Before she married Charles [my stepfather], only my mother would encourage me and try to make me feel good. That dependency was transferred to my spouse after we were married. And then my perspective on that verse in Scripture about "being obedient to your husband" (see 1 Peter 3:1) came into play. I tried to please him in every way I knew how. He was the teacher; I was the student. He taught me proper etiquette. He taught me how to cook. He taught me to decorate the house to his liking. He did everything so well that there was no way I could match his talents. He was so smart and everyone loved him.

When the little doubts would pop into my head, I just hid them. Maybe I ignored them. I didn't want anything to mar the family picture, so I chose not to believe any of the doubts. Christians are supposed to be positive, joyful people. For that reason, I would strive to show only the good, the happy, the beautiful. Smile away the frowns, the tears, the inner pain. Hide behind the mask.

He and his behavior totally controlled my life. I allowed situations to go on even though I questioned his faithfulness. It caused me to tolerate many things that I should have put a stop to years before.[6]

Even when it became apparent that my husband had no intentions of renouncing his lifestyle, I was resistant to getting a divorce. I kept believing that it would work out—that God would take care of the situation. But the underlying cause of my hesitation to file for divorce was my codependency: I didn't believe I could function in the natural without him. It was like trying to quit smoking cold turkey. I was "addicted" to my husband, and without him I felt abandoned, unsupported, incompetent, and lost. I felt as if my identity had been stripped away.

---

[6]Hunter, *Healing the Heart*, 114–115.

Meanwhile, I was still helping in my parents' ministry, even as my heart ached from the gaping hole created by my husband's absence.

> *Codependency is an illness that distorts your vision and eats away at your self-image.*

Codependency is an illness that distorts your vision and eats away at your self-image. Yet many people fail to escape this illness because they'd rather put up with bondage and enjoy its "benefits," as I did for a while—after all, it was good to have a roof over my head and to have all of my physical needs met. But the pain of separation from my husband was worth it, because it forced me to find myself and, more important, to put God in His proper place in my life: first place.

Someone who is codependent essentially makes another person the god of his or her life—a higher being without whom he or she cannot survive. And this accounts for the reason so many victims of abuse return to their "vomit"—go back to their abusers.

ESCAPE THE PAST

Years ago, I gave a talk on the distractions that keep us from doing all that we have been called to do. To provide a visual illustration—see if you can imagine it—I wore an electric-blue wig on my head, a bright-orange boa around my neck, and a bandage on my right arm. I also had bare feet. (I was a sight to behold.) I held a tube of lipstick in one hand and a rearview mirror in the other. It sounds like a disjointed ensemble, I know, but each element symbolized a specific source of distraction in our lives.

The blue wig represented the process of becoming so stressed that our hair turns gray or even falls out. The boa was meant to show what happens when we become financially strapped and debt wraps itself like a boa constrictor around our necks. The tube of lipstick represented pride, which often gets in the way of what God wants us to do. The bandage on my arm was to symbolize failing health, which causes many people to wonder how God could ever use them. The lack of shoes stood for lack in general: lack of experience, lack of education, lack of expertise—any perceived lack that we believe stands in the way of our achieving anything. Finally, the rearview mirror was to represent the past—where we have come from.

Is your past holding you back? Let's explore the symbolism of the rearview mirror a little more. As you are driving along, if you keep your focus on your rearview mirror, you won't get very far before you run into something—or someone. It doesn't hurt to glance in the rearview every once in a while, but it's dangerous to concentrate on it exclusively. Likewise, while it's useful to keep an eye on certain parts of your past, dwelling entirely on where you've been can become a major deterrent that keeps you from doing what God has called you to do. It becomes like a ball and chain, holding you prisoner—when you're holding the key!

You may think that God can't use you because of any number of reasons. Maybe you have said something like, "God can't use me—I got a divorce," or "God can't use me—I've done some pretty terrible things." Whatever your reasons, they're the exact reason God *wants to* and *will* use you! He can use you because His Son died on the cross to forgive your sins and to set you free from your past—past hurts, past wrongdoings, past traumas, and so forth. You have been made clean and pure through His precious blood, by which He purchased you—all of you, your past included. Release it to Him; it no longer belongs to you. Hallelujah!

RESIST RETURNING TO HARMFUL HABITS

Many times, people who have come from a different kind of lifestyle have had traumas in their lives—abandonment, abuse, and so forth—turn to drugs, alcohol, sex, pornography, and other things to help ease the pain.

I know a man and a woman with similar stories. Both were abused by men and subsequently abandoned by their parents, who refused to believe their reports of abuse. As a result, they turned to an alternative lifestyle.

Both this man and this woman were dear to my heart. I worked with them to help them find freedom from this lifestyle they had chosen, and they did find a measure of deliverance. I also encouraged them to seek professional counsel. Yet both insisted they were fine and didn't need any help.

Meanwhile, they continued to spend time with members of the same sex who had struggled in the same area. I warned them, "You're playing with fire." I went on to explain that the enemy desperately wanted to drag them back into the lifestyle they said they were trying to leave behind. I also cautioned them not to be alone with another person. To avoid temptation of any kind, they needed to socialize with a group of friends, not just one.

Both of them assured me that they would never return to that lifestyle. And yet, at the time of this writing, both of them are back where they started, following the lifestyle they swore they'd leave behind. And it broke my heart to hear them admit that they *knew what they were doing* when they went back to that lifestyle.

Their situation reminds me of a comment I once heard: "You can choose your sin, but you cannot choose your consequences." Neither one of them thought it would cost so much! The decision to return to the lifestyle they had temporarily left behind ended up costing them their jobs, their families, and their friendships, and it kept them from fulfilling what God had called them to do.

I want you to understand: the decision to change is up to each of us as individuals. If you're the one who's trying to break free of a harmful habit or self-destructive lifestyle, you need to make the decision for yourself. If you're trying to help someone else to break away from a harmful habit, remember that the ultimate outcome isn't up to you. That person will choose whether or not to accept your loving counsel. Do not feel undue responsibility for others' deliverance.

PRACTICAL STEPS TO STAYING FREE

+ Guard your heart.

  Above all else, guard your heart, for it is the wellspring of life.

  (Proverbs 4:23)

+ Cast down "imaginations."

  For though we walk in the flesh, we do not war after the flesh: (for the weapons of our warfare are not carnal, but mighty through God to the pulling down of strong holds;) casting down imaginations, and every high thing that exalteth itself against the knowledge of God, and bringing into captivity every thought to the obedience of Christ.

+ Flee from evil.

   Flee the evil desires of youth, and pursue righteousness, faith, love and peace, along with those who call on the Lord out of a pure heart.
   (2 Timothy 2:22)

+ Know the truth, which will set you free.

   [Jesus said,] *"If you hold to my teaching, you are really my disciples. Then you will know the truth, and the truth will set you free."*
   (John 8:31–32)

+ Know your vulnerabilities and determine not to let the enemy steal your testimony.

   The thief comes only to steal and kill and destroy. (John 10:10)

   They overcame him [Satan] by the blood of the Lamb and by the word of their testimony. (Revelation 12:11)

+ Avoid spending time with people who are engaged in the very practices you're trying to cast off.
+ If you are meeting with someone to minister to him or her or to receive ministry yourself, select a public place. Whenever I minister to a person of the opposite sex, I leave the door open or have someone in the room with me.
+ Renounce any unholy covenants that you have made with anyone.
+ Listen to those around you who have your best interests in mind. Heed godly advice. Listen to what your pastor tells you. Pay attention to your spouse. Otherwise, you may know what you shouldn't do but do it, anyway. The man and the woman I mentioned earlier "knew" they were strong enough to resist their former lifestyle but fell right back into it! I have an acquaintance who had been addicted to alcohol for a time. Some of his friends invited him over, and his wife said, "Don't go. I feel this is a setup from the enemy." He went anyway—alone—and ended up getting pulled back into a drinking

habit. While he was under the influence, he was used as a scapegoat for a crime—a serious way of paying for his mistake.

Get free and stay free!

Scriptures to Take to Heart

What benefit did you reap at that time from the things you are now ashamed of? Those things result in death! But now that you have been set free from sin and have become slaves to God, the benefit you reap leads to holiness, and the result is eternal life. (Romans 6:21–22)

You were taught, with regard to your former way of life, to put off your old self, which is being corrupted by its deceitful desires; to be made new in the attitude of your minds; and to put on the new self, created to be like God in true righteousness and holiness. (Ephesians 4:22–24)

Anyone who listens to the word but does not do what it says is like a man who looks at his face in a mirror and, after looking at himself, goes away and immediately forgets what he looks like. But the man who looks intently into the perfect law that gives freedom, and continues to do this, not forgetting what he has heard, but doing it—he will be blessed in what he does. (James 1:23–25)

CHAPTER 7

Discover Your True Identity

Once you have cast off the pain of your past, it's time to move forward and step into your true identity. But that assumes you know your true identity. As an introduction to this topic, let's turn to John 1:19–23:

> Now this is the testimony of John, when the Jews sent priests and Levites from Jerusalem to ask him, "Who are you?" He confessed, and did not deny, but confessed, "I am not the Christ." And they asked him, "What then? Are you Elijah?" He said, "I am not." "Are you the Prophet?" And he answered, "No." Then they said to him, "Who are you, that we may give an answer to those who sent us? What do you say about yourself?" He said: "I am 'The voice of one crying in the wilderness: "Make straight the way of the LORD,"'" as the prophet Isaiah said.　　　(NKJV)

We see from this passage that John the Baptist knew who he wasn't, and he also knew who he was. Part of knowing who you are is knowing who you are *not*.

In this chapter, we are going to help you answer the question "Who am I?" Our goal is to discover your true identity—not just your identity according to the Bible, which calls you *"the righteousness of God"* (2 Corinthians 5:21) and *"the head, not the tail…at the top, never at the bottom"* (Deuteronomy 28:13). Those are aspects of who you are in Christ, but I want to talk about who you *really* are, underneath everything else, at your very core.

AN IDENTITY CRISIS

I'll never forget the identity crisis I went through at forty-six years of age. I was divorced after twenty-five years of marriage, and all four of my daughters had grown up and gone off to college or embarked on a missions trip, so there was nobody home with me except the dogs. When it was time to decide what to cook for dinner or to make another similarly insignificant decision, I found myself stuck. I was unable to answer the question "What do I want for dinner?" I didn't know what I wanted to eat, much less what I wanted for the rest of my life. And I certainly didn't know who I was.

Defined by Other People

Many people know me as the daughter of Charles and Frances Hunter. For years and years, I got my identity from my parents, who were well-known for their healing ministry. Whenever I met someone, it was always, "I'm the Hunters' daughter."

Then, when I got married, my identity took on an additional tag; I was "his wife." When we started having children, I became "Melody's mom," "Charity's mom," "Spice's mom," and "Abigail's mom."

I didn't resent those titles, by any means, but I didn't know who I was unless there was someone around to give me an identity. As a result, my self-esteem was incredibly low. I had no sense of myself, apart from my relation to the people in my life. I had no clue what I wanted to do or who I wanted to be. I knew I wanted to be a good wife, a good mother, and a good daughter—and I was. But I didn't know who I was if those roles were to be stripped away. Maybe you can relate.

Fulfilling the Descriptions of Others

As I mentioned in an earlier chapter, in my growing-up years, I didn't receive a lot of positive affirmation. I was told that I was "retarded" and "dumb," that I would never accomplish anything, that I was morbidly obese and ugly, and so on. And, as often happens, the comments I consistently heard became self-fulfilling prophecies. We tend to take on the attributes people ascribe to us, whether they are valid or not.

I don't want to be defined by the people in my life. I don't want to be the "stupid" or "ugly" person who would "never amount to anything." How many times have you agreed with negative statements about you? How often do you find yourself saying, for example, "Yeah, you're right, I'll never accomplish anything. No wonder I made another mistake." I can't tell you how many times I've said that about myself—"They were right; I can't do anything." I received a steady stream of verbal abuse and put-downs from

We tend to take on the attributes people ascribe to us, whether they are valid or not.

my peers and certain relatives (but, again, never from my parents, mind you), and it was a huge challenge to overcome. For a while, I believed them, and so I never put forth much effort, if any, at school. At home, I was told, "You can't clean the house worth anything," and so I didn't even try. And, through my lack of effort, I proved them right. I allowed their negative words to be prophetic.

Eventually, I surrendered my negative self-image and laid it on God's altar. I chose to stop serving others' opinions of me and the painful memories of my past and to start serving the Lord.

Every day, we have to choose whom or what we're going to serve. It isn't a onetime decision; it's a choice we must make on a daily basis.

Imitating Excessively

A lot of preachers don't know who they are, and so they try to emulate other preachers' styles, so much so that they earn nicknames based on whom they're modeling—for example, there are "Haginites" (people who preach like Kenneth Hagin) and "Copelandites" (people who preach in the style of Kenneth Copeland). Now, all of us have role models and mentors we desire to emulate, but we shouldn't get to the point where we try to become them. Through the years, especially as my parents got older, people would tell me, "You need to start acting more like your mother. You ought to practice her mannerisms." No disrespect, but, to quote my mom, "God says that one Frances Hunter is enough, or He would have made two." God also says that one Joan Hunter is enough.

Anyway, whenever I would listen to this type of advice and decide, "Well, I could probably afford to be a little more like Mom in this mannerism," God would rebuke me and say, "Are you going to be like her or like Me?" Then, I would say, "Excuse me, Father. I want to be like You." We need to cultivate the attributes of God. I can't tell you how many people have told me, "You are a Frances Hunter." I'm not a Frances Hunter! I may have a lot of similarities with my mom, but God doesn't want me to be another Frances Hunter. He wants me to be Joan Hunter.

And God wants you to be you. That's why He created you with a custom design! Each of us is unique. God numbers the hairs on our heads (see Matthew 10:30; Luke 12:7), and no two people have the same fingerprints. We should embrace our distinctiveness, not seek to take on somebody else's.

Who Am I?

Let's start with a simple exercise. On a piece of paper, start to make a list of answers to the question "Who am I?" Don't write, "I work for so-and-so," "I am a mother," "I am a father," "I was the valedictorian of my class," or other accomplishments. The question is not "What do you do?" or "What have you done?" but "Who are you?"

Many years ago, I was praying to God and asking for wisdom in various situations in my life. Number one, I was trying to figure out who I was. This was at the time I would get stuck wondering what to make for dinner, a situation I talked about at the beginning of this chapter. I started making decisions for myself—what dishes to prepare, how to style my hair, and so forth. For years, I had kept my hair long because it had seemed expected of me. Soon, I realized that I wanted to try something different, so I cut my hair short. It was a liberating experience.

I made some other changes, admittedly due in part to the opinions of others. One thing people always complimented me on was my eyes. They would say, "Your best feature is your eyes," and I would think, *Well, I may look like a balloon and be morbidly obese, but at least I have good-looking eyes.* I ended up losing weight, but I also focused on my eyes: always wearing mascara and other eye makeup and even having LASIK surgery to eliminate the need to wear big, thick eyeglasses.

I chose to accentuate the positive. For example, I often wear blue shirts and apply eye shadow to bring out the blue in my eyes. We can highlight our positive attributes and focus on those rather than the areas others think we need to work on. Everyone always talks about how we should focus on our inner beauty, and that's true, but we can also be thankful for our outward beauty.

So, as you make your list, think about your positive physical attributes. Don't just write, "I think I'm beautiful"; say, "I know I'm beautiful!" For many people, that's difficult to say. The first time I uttered those words, it felt as if a boulder was stuck in my throat because I had always been told otherwise. The exception was my mom; she would tell me, "You're so beautiful," and I would reply, "You have to say that because you're my mom."

> *You need to change your perception of yourself so that it matches God's perception of you.*

I want you to take a look in the mirror and, if possible, write down on that mirror who you are with a dry-erase marker. On my mirror at home, I have written, "I am loving." Anyone who has ever seen me as a mother, as a wife, as a minister, and as a friend knows I am loving. I'm a giver; I'm sincere; I'm a servant; I'm a friend; I am beautiful. Pretty soon, you'll run out of space to write!

You need to change your perception of yourself so that it matches God's perception of you. Some people might say, "I'm too busy to think about myself." That's being selfish! I believe God wants us to think about ourselves more than we do, because how else can we evaluate our spiritual disciplines and go about reordering our lives so that they align more closely with His purposes? We need to think about ourselves and assess whether we're eating enough (or too much), whether we're getting adequate rest, whether we're exercising enough, whether we're spending enough time in the Word of God, and so forth.

We need to find out who we are so that we may develop our character, our faith, and other aspects of ourselves.

I was looking at some pictures the other day, and one of them really struck me. It's a picture of a young woman who's lost—who doesn't know who she is. She knew who she was in Christ, but she was clueless about her core identity. They say that the eyes are the window to the soul, and her eyes revealed her lack of self-awareness. At that point, she started turning to food to fill the void in her life. And I looked at that photo the other day and said, "Thank You, God, for the grace that You give." Then, I looked at another picture of the same woman, taken a few years later, when she had figured out who she was—when I figured out who I was!

When the photographer had taken this picture, he'd said to me, "There is something about your eyes. In my twenty-one years of experience in the photography business, I've never seen eyes like yours. They sparkle, like in a Disney movie." Those were the eyes of somebody who knew who she was. Somebody who sparkled with the love of Jesus Christ in her heart. Somebody who knew that God had called her and set her apart and protected her through the years. Somebody who doesn't just think that she's beautiful but knows it, and not with a sense of pride or egotism.

STOP BELIEVING THE LIE

A lot of your identity is founded on what other people have said about you or even done to you. Often, you may feel responsible for things that happen to you when someone else is to blame. You believe that you did whatever it was, and you reap the guilt and self-blame that should belong to someone else.

I have ministered to many people who were suffering from misplaced guilt and mistaken responsibility. Let me share an example.

An eighty-three-year-old woman came to me for prayer. She told me she wanted to get free of the guilt she felt for having made a fifty-plus-year-old man, who was a friend of the family, molest her when she was three.

"What?" I couldn't believe she'd been carrying a sense of guilt and shame for that situation for eighty years.

She repeated her request.

I then asked her what she had done to make this man molest her.

She said, "I had a dress on, and I was dancing all around him, like any little girl might do. And then it happened."

I asked her again, "What did you do?" I wanted her to take a good look at the situation and analyze it.

She repeated what she'd said before about dancing around in a dress.

I then asked her the same question, but from a different angle. I pointed to a young girl in attendance who looked to be about three years old, and I said, "What could that sweet little three-year-old girl over there do to make a grown man do something like that to her? Really, what could she do?"

"Nothing," she admitted.

"Okay, but what about you?"

I let her digest that question before I asked her another one: "What you have believed about what happened to you—is it the truth, or is it a lie?"

"A lie."

I instructed her to repeat after me: "I have been believing a lie."

She did as I asked.

"Louder!" I said.

"I have been believing a lie."

"Again!"

"I have been believing a lie!"

I asked her to keep saying that until she truly believed it was a lie.

She did. And she was set free.

What lies has the enemy been whispering to you? What deceptions has the devil been leading you to believe? Has he been calling you "dumb"? "Stupid"? "Ugly"? "Clumsy"? "Weak"? Has he caused you to feel at fault for a situation over which you had as much control as a three-year-old?

If so, start saying out loud, "I have been believing a lie." Say it until you mean it!

Get free of all the lies, for only then can you begin to believe the truth about yourself and come to accept—and even love—yourself.

Here is another testimony from a woman whose life was changed when her eyes were opened to the false responsibility she'd been carrying for years:

> In your teaching on false responsibility, you touched on a very important part of my life. I was molested by my dad when I was nine. So was my sister. I have a long story, one that I will not get into at this time, because I know your time is precious, but I did forgive him to his face, after I was grown and married.
>
> When you spoke on false responsibility, you said something that really struck me: "It's not your fault." I had never thought of it that way before. I had always thought it was because I had been "fully developed" at the age of nine.
>
> After all these years, I finally realized that God released me of all of the condemnation I had been putting on myself. I thank God that He sent you with this wonderful message, and I can't wait to share it with my sister, who desperately needs to hear that it's not our fault!
>
> I led my dad to Jesus on May 20, 1999. He passed away last year. During this teaching, I felt released.
>
> *Thank you,*
> *Your sister in Christ*

LEARNING TO LOVE YOURSELF

I remember ministering to a man who had no clue how to love his wife. He said to me, "How can I love my wife if I don't even love myself?" It was a valid question. How can you love your spouse if you don't first love yourself? How can you love other people to whom you minister if you don't love yourself? If you don't know who you are, you are not ministering from a standpoint that desires to see them become all they can be. Loving ourselves is the only way to fulfill what Jesus identified as the most important commandments when He said,

"Love the Lord your God with all your heart and with all your soul and with all your mind." This is the first and greatest commandment. And the second is like it: "Love your neighbor as yourself." All the Law and the Prophets hang on these two commandments. (Matthew 22:37–40)

I can speak and minister day after day because I know I am loved by God, and no one can take that away from me.

For I am convinced that neither death nor life, neither angels nor demons, neither the present nor the future, nor any powers, neither height nor depth, nor anything else in all creation, will be able to separate us from the love of God that is in Christ Jesus our Lord. (Romans 8:38–39)

For that reason, I can travel around the world and minister with a sense of confidence in who I am.

When I was in my late teens and early twenties, traveling in ministry with my mom and dad, I had such low self-esteem that I thought I couldn't do anything. I felt I was worthless compared to my parents. After all, anyone with the choice of having one of the three of us pray for them would usually go to my mom. So, I'd sit in the back while she ministered, or I'd hide behind the darkest curtain I could find and stay secluded because I didn't count myself worthy of being seen. However, my mom would find me every time, drag me out, and force me to shake hands with the people. I knew they couldn't have cared less if they shook my hand, but at least she got me out from behind the curtain.

Some of you are hiding behind a curtain today. It's evident in your stance—how you carry yourself. And you can recognize it in other people, as well. They'll do whatever they can to hide their face, their mouth, or their eyes, either literally or figuratively, through silence, for example. I don't hide my eyes anymore, because they have the sparkle of Jesus Christ. Today, I can minister to anyone, anywhere—grocery stores, airports, and so forth—because I no longer fear rejection. Jesus Christ took my rejection to the cross, and now I don't have to suffer from it anymore. He took my pain to the cross, too, with the same effect. He knew who He was, and He wants us to discover our identities, as well.

Be Comfortable in Your Own Skin

In this earthly life, "stuff" happens. A dysfunctional family has become the norm nowadays. That's the state of things due to demonic activity and satanic influences through television, drugs and alcohol, stress, broken families, and so on. Unfortunately, there are many factors related to dysfunctional families that contribute to people's sense of worthlessness. I know a woman who was molested at five years of age. She was seventy years old when I met her, and, similar to the eighty-three-year-old woman whose story I told earlier, she was still convinced that it had been her fault that the man had molested her. Living decade after decade with such a strong sense of guilt had ruined her marriage and inhibited her ability to function in society. She had been living a lie. And it's a shame that it took so long for her to be delivered from the sense of self-blame.

As I've said, it took me a while to stop living the lies others told me—believing I was "retarded" and "stupid"; thinking I would remain morbidly obese for life and that dieting was pointless; blaming myself for the time when my uncle molested me. I needed to accept the call of God on my life and to stop comparing myself with my parents and their legacy. I'm not supposed to compare myself with Charles and Frances Hunter. I thank God they're my mom and dad, but I will never be them—nor am I supposed to be. Again, I am to be the best me that I can ever be. And I want to make constant strides toward bettering myself. Am I perfect? No. But perfection is my goal. I want to be a better and more anointed minister of God than ever before. I want my relationship with God to grow day by day, so that I am continually moving closer to Him.

Be Convinced of Your Own Beauty

Some time ago, I was on my way to New York State to speak at a large convention. I made it, and so did my teaching CDs—but that was about it. My clothes didn't make it, my makeup didn't make it, my jewelry didn't make it, my shoes didn't make it, and my toothbrush didn't make it. What an inconvenience! It was humbling, too, since I had to purchase a dress for a formal event on Sunday evening, and the only store around was a superstore. I wasn't completely crushed, because clothing is not my god, however I was very disappointed about losing the Bible I'd had for thirty-plus years.

When I got up to minister at the formal banquet, the anointing upon me was strong. Yet I didn't feel extremely comfortable in the clothes I was wearing. My outfit hardly qualified as even business casual. I also felt extremely mismatched, since I am accustomed to dressing with a theme and coordinating my accessories, clothing, and shoes.

But God used this experience to teach me that it isn't my clothes that make me beautiful. Whether I'm wearing a pretty, feminine cardigan or a pair of jeans and an old T-shirt, I'm beautiful. God said to me, "You are beautiful, with or without your yellow suit or your turquoise pants outfit." (That was my dad's favorite outfit on me.) Nice clothes make me feel good—there's no doubt about that. So does perfume. I like to smell good, to look good, and to feel good. I never go out of the house without first putting on makeup. Even if I'm just running out to check the mail, I'll apply makeup in order to look my best—because looking good makes me *feel* good. It activates a cycle, too: the better you feel about yourself, the more you want to make yourself look good, and so on.

> *Whether I'm wearing a pretty, feminine cardigan or a pair of jeans and an old T-shirt, I'm beautiful.*

Weeks passed. The airline couldn't locate my missing suitcase. I finally received a phone call from the airline informing me there was no hope of finding my belongings. I was thankful for the sense of closure, even though I felt disappointed, once again. However, I am confident that everything happens for a reason: to bring glory to God. I reflected on the possible reasons for why my suitcase was lost. I remembered what God told me that day. I was at peace and blessed the person who received the items that were once so valuable to me.

A few years ago, I recognized an old friend of mine who had been a classmate at Oral Roberts University. I said, "Hi, Ben!" and gave him a big hug. He looked alarmed—obviously, he didn't recognize me. So,

I stepped back and said, "Ben, it's Joan." His eyes widened. "My Joan?" "Yes." "Oh!" he exclaimed as he gave me a hug. I don't blame him for failing to recognize me. After all, I had lost a lot of weight, undergone LASIK surgery, gotten my hair cut short, and made a variety of other changes. I had also experienced forgiveness and healing, which always radiate on the outside, especially in the eyes.

Don't Be So Hard on Yourself

I love ministering to people and witnessing the change in their eyes. It's so exciting to see their eyes light up and sparkle with the light of the love of Jesus Christ. All of us have had things spoken over us through the years, many of them not so good. But I can always tell who's been the hardest on each person: himself or herself. We are our worst critics. I've had to deal with the put-downs that have come from myself more than any put-downs from anyone else. The childhood epigram "Sticks and stones may break my bones, but words will never hurt me" is the biggest lie I've ever heard. In most cases, words hurt far more than any physical force. Words pierce and penetrate to our very core.

Speak Positive Words over Yourself and Others

The power of words is true of negative and positive words alike, which is why verbal affirmation is so important. Years ago, a particular airline received one of the lowest ratings of customer service, and the company was preparing to file bankruptcy. Then, a new president took office, and he went around telling all of the employees what a good job they were doing. Today, that airline consistently earns one of the highest ratings in the nation, all because of the power of positive words of affirmation spoken over its employees.

If you're an employer, speak positive words over your employees. If a parent, speak positive words over your children. If a husband or wife, speak positive words over your spouse. You may need to make these confessions in faith, trusting that God will bring them to pass, such as: "My children are taught of the Lord, and great is their peace, in the name of Jesus. I have brought them up in the admonition of the Lord, and when they have grown, they will not depart from my teachings."

(See Isaiah 54:13; Proverbs 22:6.) Confess something of that nature over your children, both in the privacy of your personal prayer time and in their presence or over the phone to them. Tell them, "You are highly favored of the Lord." When you speak positive things over your children, it gives them a desire to love the Lord and to strive to do better and better—to accomplish greater and greater things.

So, speak in a positive way to yourself and others. Tell yourself, "I am beautiful." Speak those words to your reflection in the mirror. It isn't enough to hear other people say, "You're beautiful." You need to agree with them. You need to see what they see—and to see it with your heart.

Love Yourself

A few years ago, a lady who looked overweight came to one of our services. I passed her on the way in and noticed that she was comparing the size of her stomach with that of another woman. The difference was, the other woman was pregnant, while this woman was not; she had forty-two tumors in her stomach, as I would later find out.

During the service, I received a word of knowledge about someone with tumors in the abdominal area. The woman I had seen earlier came forward. I prayed for her, and all of the tumors vanished miraculously! She actually had to buy a new pair of pants on the way home because she had lost so much mass around her waist.

Yet I could sense that the healing she needed went beyond her stomach tumors. So, I placed my hand over her heart and continued ministering to her as I cursed the spirits of trauma, abandonment, rejection, and many other things.

After several minutes, she began to cry. Pastor David called out, "I love you, Tortia!"

She said through her tears, "I love you, Pastor."

I pointed to Pastor David and then said to her, "Repeat that."

She said again, "I love you, Pastor."

I shook my head, realizing she'd misunderstood me. "No, repeat what he said."

She tried. And she started gagging. "I lov-v-v...."

"Come on," I coaxed her. "You can say it."

"I...." (Cough, cough; gag, gag.)

All the while, I held my hand to her chest as I prayed for her.

More than five minutes had passed when she finally said, "I love Tortia."

I had her repeat it till she meant it. Eventually, she was able to shout it! And then all of us were crying.

Why is it so hard to say, "I love ___(your name)___"? Say it now: "I love_____."

You may think this is silly or weird or even egotistical. But the Word commands us, "Love your neighbor as you love yourself." (See Leviticus 19:18; Matthew 19:19; 22:39; Mark 12:31, 33; Luke 10:27; Romans 13:9; Galatians 5:14; James 2:8.) Again, God wants us to love ourselves so we can love others.

I want to tell you a little more about the miracle that has unfolded in Tortia's life.

Before being delivered from self-loathing, she would wake up every morning, look in the mirror, and say, "You are so ugly!"

Throughout the day, whenever she passed a mirror, she would repeat that phrase in her mind, along with a host of other negative comments about herself.

Today, she wakes up every morning, looks in the mirror, and says, "You are so beautiful!"

Look in the mirror and say, "You are so beautiful!" or "You are so handsome!"

God created you in His image. When you see yourself as God sees you, you can't help but "fall in love."

IN THE IMAGE OF THE KING

I want to be more and more Christlike—to increase in godliness. God is loving. God is a generous giver. God never lies—He is sincere.

He is our friend, and He is a servant, ready to sacrifice for us. As Jesus' representatives on the earth, we all should desire to conform more closely to His nature.

The first step toward doing that is truly knowing who you are. When you do the exercise I gave you earlier and seek to answer the question "Who am I?" you're probably going to come up with some answers you don't like: "I am critical," "I am a perfectionist," "I am ugly," and the like. When those attributes come up, you need to lay them on the altar of God and ask Him to give you a spirit of grace instead of a critical attitude, patience instead of petulance, and so forth. Ask Him to cultivate the fruit of the Spirit in your life, and He will answer you, because He desires that you grow in those areas.

PRAYER

I want to lead you in a prayer to cast off the negative words that have been spoken over you, to release you to be who God wants you to be, and to launch you on a voyage of self-discovery. Let's pray together:

"Father, in the name of Jesus, I repent of all the words I have spoken that do not line up with who I am or with who You have called me to be. I also repent of all my actions that were contrary to what You have called me to do. Open my eyes to see the person You made me to be and the purpose for which You designed me. I repent of every word I have spoken about others that did not edify, exhort, correct in love, or confirm. I now renounce all words spoken over me that did not line up with who I truly am. I choose to be who You would have me to be—the person You had in mind when You fashioned me in my mother's womb. In Jesus' name, amen."

Scriptures to Take to Heart

For you created my inmost being; you knit me together in my mother's womb. I praise you because I am fearfully and wonderfully made; your works are wonderful, I know that full well. (Psalm 139:13–14)

Before I formed you in the womb I knew you, before you were born I set you apart; I appointed you.... (Jeremiah 1:5)

[Jesus said,] *"I no longer call you servants, because a servant does not know his master's business. Instead, I have called you friends, for everything that I learned from my Father I have made known to you. You did not choose me, but I chose you and appointed you to go and bear fruit—fruit that will last."* (John 15:15–16)

CHAPTER 8

Drawing Closer to God

My prayer for you is

that the God of our Lord Jesus Christ, the Father of glory, may give to you the spirit of wisdom and revelation in the knowledge of Him, the eyes of your understanding being enlightened; that you may know what is the hope of His calling, what are the riches of the glory of His inheritance in the saints, and what is the exceeding greatness of His power toward us who believe. (Ephesians 1:17–19 NKJV)

I pray that you would discover all that you are and all that God has for you. I pray that your experience would be like mine: receiving visions and dreams from God and then going out and living the dream. Today, I am doing exactly what God has called me to do and ministering wherever He guides me to go. Every day is an exciting new adventure. I love to lay hands on the sick and see them recover. Wherever I go, the power of God goes with me as evidence that I am walking out His plan for me.

I didn't get here overnight, however. My path to the center of God's plan took me through trials and tribulations, through plenty of mistakes—or, as I like to call them, learning experiences. I learned a lot of lessons the hard way, and now I share those lessons with others, in hopes of sparing them the same agony. I would rather learn from somebody else's mistakes and not make them myself, wouldn't you?

In the Chinese language, the symbol for the word *crisis* is made up of two other symbols: one represents "potential danger," while the other one represents "hidden opportunity." Fascinating, isn't it? The makeup of the word *crisis* essentially defines it as an event that involves risk but also provides potential—a hidden opportunity for something positive. Every crisis is what we make it. We get to decide whether it will be a danger that derails us or an opportunity for us to ascend to new heights.

MAKING SENSE OF YOUR SORROWS

At one point or another, each of us has asked the question, "Why is this happening to me?" The Bible says, *"Your enemy the devil prowls around like a roaring lion looking for someone to devour"* (1 Peter 5:8). The devil's aim is to distract us with whatever devices he can in order to keep us from fulfilling God's purposes for us. Picture a hungry lion on the prowl, and you'll know the stance of Satan toward us, the children of God, whom he wants to destroy. In a nutshell, his mission is *"only to steal and kill and destroy"* (John 10:10). And, sometimes, our old earthly nature just gets in the way. (See, for example, Colossians 3:5–10.) It is possible to find yourself in a mess of your own making. Sometimes, our sin opens the door to the devil. Maybe we visited an illicit Web site on the Internet. Maybe we've given in to another temptation. Whatever it was, it opened the door to the devil. But it doesn't have to stay that way.

I have described some of the difficulties I faced growing up and even into adulthood and have alluded to others. I've been through hell, but—praise God!—I made it through. The situations that I have encountered and overcome are what have made me who I am today and gotten me to my current position. Today, I have a strength I could not have even conceived of twenty years ago. It's a strength that has developed and matured only through trials—through fighting the good fight. Paul wrote,

> *Timothy, my son, I give you this instruction in keeping with the prophecies once made about you, so that by following them you may fight the good fight, holding on to faith and a good conscience. Some have rejected these and so have shipwrecked their faith....Fight the good fight of the faith. Take hold of the eternal life to which you were called when you made your good confession in the presence of many witnesses.*
>
> (1 Timothy 1:18–19; 6:12)

I have fought the good fight, I have finished the race, I have kept the faith. (2 Timothy 4:7)

You never fight the good fight and come out weak. Rather, through resisting trials and by relying on the Lord, you grow stronger and stronger, day by day. The better I know the Word of God, the more of His Word I have inside of me, and the better equipped I am to ward off the devil's schemes, just as Jesus did. (See, for example, Matthew 4:1–11.) And the stronger I become. I want you to be as strong as you can possibly be.

> *You never fight the good fight and come out weak.*

One of the best explanations of why horrible things happen to us can be found in 2 Corinthians 7. The context is a letter of correction that Paul had previously sent to the church at Corinth, which he had written in a strong tone and which he was following up on with them.

Paul said,

I am no longer sorry that I sent that letter to you, though I was very sorry for a time, realizing how painful it would be to you. But it hurt you only for a little while. Now I am glad I sent it, not because it hurt you but because the pain turned you to God. It was a good kind of sorrow you felt, the kind of sorrow God wants his people to have, so that I need not come to you with harshness. For God sometimes uses sorrow in our lives to help us turn away from sin and seek eternal life. We should never regret his sending it. But the sorrow of the man who is not a Christian is not the sorrow of true repentance and does not prevent eternal death. Just see how much good this grief from the Lord did for you! You no longer shrugged your shoulders but became earnest and sincere and very anxious to get rid of the sin that I wrote you about. You became frightened about what had happened and longed for me to come and help. You went right to work on the problem and cleared it up (punishing the man who sinned). You have done everything you could to make it right. (2 Corinthians 7:8–11 TLB)

God revealed to me that the letter to which Paul was referring, and about which he was explaining, can represent the difficult situation in your life. It can represent the person who hurt you or the outcome you dreaded—any source of devastation—which should cause you to turn to God.

Situations arise in our lives, and we want to know why. We want to know who's responsible. Did God send them to us? The devil? Did we bring them on ourselves? We want to know the reason. However, we are not guaranteed an answer or an explanation. Our only guarantee is that God can make a miracle out of them if we'll come to Him and trust Him to do so. He can take any negative situation and turn it around for our good. (See Genesis 50:20; Romans 8:28.)

THE LORD IS THERE IN THE MIDST OF OUR DEVASTATION

A few weeks ago, a situation happened that took me back to a horrible time in my life—a time when I was made to feel like trash, a time when I felt worthless beyond words. I had thought I had made a terrible mistake from which I would never recover. The people who were involved in this incident never apologized or showed remorse. I asked God to forgive them, for the sake of my own sanity and emotional well-being.

I also forgave those people. What they had done was devastating and sinful, but I gave it to God and put it on the cross. It has been paid for by the perfect blood of Jesus, and, on the day of judgment, it will not be held against them, either by God or by me. Through this process, I became free from the pain. But the enemy loves to remind us of the misdeeds and misfortunes of our pasts, even the ones that we've handed over to Jesus. He keeps bringing them to mind in hopes that we'll fall into a pit of despair over the atrocities that either we've committed or that have been committed against us.

This is what happened when I was reminded about how horrible that situation was. I experienced the devastation anew, and again I felt that I was worth absolutely nothing—that I was no good to anybody. Obviously, those feelings were not from God.

I want to help you get through what I've been through. I don't want you to have to go where I have been. And that's why I share my heart with you. That's why I share the details of the tragedies I have been through—so that you don't have to go through them. Or, if you are going through them now, so that you can get through them!

I didn't know what I was going to do. I cried and cried. I felt like dirt, and even thinking about all of my accomplishments could do nothing to boost my mood or make me feel better about myself. Deep down, I knew I didn't mean a thing to this group of people, and I felt completely abandoned and "rotten."

So, finally, at the end of the day, I returned home, went to my bedroom, and shut the door. There, I said, "God, I need to hear from You. I'm devastated. I've been reminded of the devastation that happened to me a few years ago, and the memory doesn't feel good at all. I know that I am worth something. Man has let me down, but You, God, have never let me down."

Man may forsake me, man may hurt me, man may speak poorly of me, but my God will never speak negatively about me. Man may believe that God could never use me because I've been divorced, but my God has never forsaken me. My God has always been there, even when nobody else was there for me. In the privacy of my bedroom, when I have been feeling more alone than ever before, God has been there with me. He has comforted me when I didn't think I could make it through another day. He has collected my tears in a bottle. (See Psalm 56:8 NKJV, KJV.) I asked Him the other day, "Why are You collecting my tears?" He said, "I'm collecting them just for restoration. For, the number of tears that you have shed in pain will be restored to you many, many times with tears of joy." Remember, *"weeping may remain for a night, but rejoicing comes in the morning"* (Psalm 30:5). I praise God for His restoration. He had also shared with me, "Just remember, they [those who had hurt me] are not the ones who called you."

GOD'S TOTAL RESTORATION PACKAGE

When I returned home the night I was feeling so devastated, I also sat down to study the Bible. Now, if you're going to go at it "randomly," make sure that you are led by the Spirit. Don't close your eyes and let your finger fall where it will and then assume God is speaking to you through whichever verses you happen to read. This method may lead you to conclude that you ought to "do likewise," based on the combination of Matthew 27:5 (*"Then* [Judas] *went away and hanged himself"*) and Luke 10:37 (*"Go and do likewise"*). That isn't the way to read the Bible!

That night, I opened my Bible to the book of Ephesians, but the Lord said to me, "No, I want you to go to Joel." I said, "Okay!" because, though you may argue with God all you want, you'll never win the argument. I turned to Joel chapter 2 and read this passage:

[God] *will reply, "See, I am sending you much corn and wine and oil, to fully satisfy your need. No longer will I make you a laughingstock among the nations. I will remove these armies from the north and send them far away; I will turn them back into the parched wastelands where they will die; half shall be driven into the Dead Sea and the rest into the Mediterranean, and then their rotting stench will rise upon the land. The Lord has done a mighty miracle for you." Fear not, my people; be glad now and rejoice, for he has done amazing things for you. Let the flocks and herds forget their hunger; the pastures will turn green again. The trees will bear their fruit; the fig trees and grape vines will flourish once more. Rejoice, O people of Jerusalem, rejoice in the Lord your God! For the rains he sends are tokens of forgiveness. Once more the autumn rains will come, as well as those of spring. The threshing floors will pile high again with wheat, and the presses overflow with olive oil and wine. "And I will give you back the crops the locusts ate!—my great destroying army that I sent against you. Once again you will have all the food you want. Praise the Lord, who does these miracles for you. Never again will my people experience disaster such as this. And you will know that I am here among my people Israel, and that I alone am the Lord your God. And my people shall never again be dealt a blow like this. After I have poured out my rains again, I will pour out my Spirit upon all of you! Your sons and daughters will prophesy; your old men will dream dreams, and your young men see visions. And I will pour out my Spirit even on your slaves, men and women alike, and put strange symbols in the earth and sky—blood and fire and pillars of smoke. The sun will be turned into darkness and the moon to blood before the great and terrible*

Day of the Lord shall come. Everyone who calls upon the name of the Lord will be saved; even in Jerusalem some will escape, just as the Lord has promised, for he has chosen some to survive. At that time, when I restore the prosperity of Judah and Jerusalem," says the Lord....

(Joel 2:19–3:1 TLB)

I am not satisfied with where I am in the ministry. I am not satisfied with the anointing that flows in my life. Granted, it flows with a magnitude that makes me stand in awe of God's power, but I'm not satisfied enough to stop at this level.

Even more awe-inspiring is God's promise to ward off my enemies—to thwart any devastation that's coming my way. Through the above passage, He was telling me, "Fear not, Joan; be glad and rejoice, for I have done amazing things for you. Forget the pain; the pastures will turn green again. The trees will bear their fruit once again. Rejoice, Joan—rejoice in the Lord your God, for the rains He sends are tokens of forgiveness. The wheat harvest will be great, and the presses will overflow with olive oil and wine—you'll have an abundance of financial blessings, which you will be able to use to fund ministry trips to Israel, Ireland, Haiti, and all over. And then, I will give you back the crops that the locust ate. Anything that has been taken away, whether money or something else, I will restore to you. I will repay you for all of the devastation you have experienced. And the payback will be greater than what you originally possessed. You will have all the food you could possibly want, and the proof will be in your pockets, which will bulge not with body fat but with money and resources."

Praise the Lord, who does these miracles for us! I had received a fresh assurance that I would never experience such utter devastation again. And the same is true for you, as long as you trust in Him. God speaks to us through His written Word to let us know that He is among us and that we can trust Him to provide for and protect us, to prevent other people and life's circumstances from dealing us blow after blow.

And then, He promises to pour out His Spirit upon us—ourselves, our families, our ministries, and so forth. He will send His anointing. He will restore our prosperity—hallelujah! God is raising you and me up for such a time as this. I have no doubt about that.

GOD MISSES YOU

Several of Jesus' disciples have nicknames—there's Thomas the doubter, Peter the rock, and John the Beloved Disciple. Actually, each of us is the "Beloved Disciple." I am Joan the Beloved, and I am secure in my relationship with God, just as I am secure in the love of my parents. I always knew how proud they were of me. I want you to feel secure in the love of God, too.

I was fascinated by the late Princess Diana. I found her to be one of the most beautiful women I'd ever seen. Much of her early life was a Cinderella story, but it didn't stay that way, as you probably know, and she met her end in a tragic way. I've read a lot of material on her— books, magazine articles, and so forth. I stayed up all night to watch her funeral procession because she had touched my heart.

Now, if I had run into Princess Diana on the street, even though I felt as if I knew her, I would have refrained from running up to her and giving her a big hug. Why? Because, even though I knew all about her, I didn't really *know* her. And she would have had no clue who I was. We did not have a relationship.

Contrast that with my relationship with each of my four daughters. I have known them for their entire lives, and we have an intimate relationship. We know almost everything there is to know about each other; there are no secrets between us. We spend time together, and we communicate all of the time, either on our cell phones or with our computers.

That's how we are to relate to God. We aren't supposed to merely know everything there is to know *about* Him—we're to *know* Him personally, intimately, through a close relationship. Otherwise, when judgment day arrives, Jesus will say, "I never knew you," and we won't have the privilege of spending eternity with Him.

[Jesus said,] *"Not everyone who says to me, 'Lord, Lord,' will enter the kingdom of heaven, but only he who does the will of my Father who is in heaven. Many will say to me on that day, 'Lord, Lord, did we not prophesy in your name, and in your name drive out demons and perform many miracles?' Then I will tell them plainly, 'I never knew you. Away from me, you evildoers!'"* (Matthew 7:21–23)

I want to see Jesus running out to greet me and to welcome me to my eternal home. I want to hear Him say, "I've been waiting for you. Well done, good and faithful servant!" (See Matthew 25:21, 23.) And these things will happen because of the intimate relationship I am developing with Him during my days on the earth.

I had an intimate relationship with my earthly father, Charles Hunter. Whenever we got together, he would greet me with arms raised and fingers wiggling. Even in his later years, when he was growing weary, he would reach out his arms and beckon me to come to him. He was always eager for me to come give him a hug and a kiss. And our heavenly Father is the same way—He jumps up and down with excitement when we seek His face.

A lot of people use the words *intimacy* and *intimate* only in the context of a sexual relationship. But they mean so much more than that. In fact, sexual intimacy isn't even mentioned in the dictionary definition! In *Merriam-Webster's 11ᵗʰ Collegiate Dictionary*, the entry for *intimate* reads as follows:

1 a : INTRINSIC, ESSENTIAL b : belonging to or characterizing
    one's deepest nature
2 : marked by very close association, contact, or familiarity
3 a : marked by a warm friendship developing through long
    association b : suggesting informal warmth or privacy
4 : of a very personal or private nature

Being intimate means being close, which is part of sex, of course, but it doesn't necessarily involve a physical connection of that nature.

One day, I was worshipping the Lord during a church service when I looked up and said, "God, I have missed our time together. I've been so busy lately, always traveling, and I've missed just spending time at home with You—reading Your Word, absorbing Your wisdom, and just listening to You." I started weeping, and I heard the still, small voice whisper back, "I've missed My time with you, too." God is missing you, too.

If you are driving in a car and you have a passenger in the backseat, don't you turn your head from time to time to look back at him or her? It's instinctual to desire face-to-face communication. And that should apply to our interactions with God, as well.

It's hard on my daughters and me when we haven't seen one another in a while. Whenever I have time off for a few days in a row, I like to go visit one of my daughters. Talking on the phone is not enough if we plan to cultivate intimacy and keep our relationships flourishing. My desire to spend time with my children is nothing compared to God's desire to spend time with you and me—His children. So, as important as it is to spend quality time with those we love, what is even more crucial is spending time with God. We can't just flip through our Bibles for five minutes and call it a day. There's a time to turn off the phone, to shut down the computer, and to separate yourself so that you may give God your undivided attention.

> *Face-to-face communication should apply to our interactions with God, as well.*

It's preferable, if you're married, that the two of you communicate with God together as well as individually. Most homes have multiple bedrooms. An extra bedroom, a guest room, an office, a den, or another room may be used as a private place to pray. Spend time with God. If your spouse is not a distraction to your communication with God, then spend time reading the Word together, praying together, and coming together in unity and then watching Him move on your behalf.

It's a source of despair when your spouse stops wanting to spend time with you. I don't want that kind of relationship with my husband or with God. I want my relationship with God to be characterized by a mutual desire to be together 24/7. Whether I'm with Him one-on-one or whether my husband or children are there, He is truly there, working His will. How colorful and brilliant God is! I want to know His every angle.

In boot camp in the military, the first thing they teach you is total obedience. They don't ask for your opinion. And the Lord is the same way. He wants us to be totally obedient. Obeying becomes easier as we get to know God better, because that's how we come to love Him and to trust Him. And the more we know Him, the more we want to know Him. I know Him better now that I ever have, and better days are coming. And see, my past—my painful history—is gone. All I have are present and future. Don't worry about your history. Be healed right now, in the name of Jesus.

I want to give you the opportunity to receive Jesus Christ as your Lord and Savior, if you haven't already done so. That's where our relationship with God begins. And, even if you have already accepted Christ and entered into a relationship with God, it's never a bad idea to reaffirm your commitment to Him.

PRAY WITH ME

If you are accepting Christ for the first time, say this prayer:

"Father, I want to know You more—with greater intimacy than I ever thought possible. Jesus, I ask You to come into my life. Forgive me of my sins. Take them from me and put them on the cross, so that, on the day of judgment, You will hold no accusations against me. And, Jesus, I ask You to become the Lord of my life. Father, through Your Holy Spirit, lead me and guide me in all that You have for me to do. I surrender my life to You. In Jesus' name, amen."

Next, let's all pray the following:

"Father, right now, in the name of Jesus, I thank You for preparing my heart to receive this message. Father, thank You that You desire to have an intimate relationship with each one of us. I thank You that we're embarking on the greatest relationship we could ever fathom. Father, I am so excited to get to know You better and to enrich my relationship with You. I thank You that our relationship is going to grow by leaps and bounds. In Jesus' name, amen."

Scriptures to Take to Heart

Then you will call upon me and come and pray to me, and I will listen to you. You will seek me and find me when you seek me with all your heart.   (Jeremiah 29:12–13)

Let us draw near to God with a sincere heart in full assurance of faith, having our hearts sprinkled to cleanse us from a guilty conscience and having our bodies washed with pure water. Let us hold unswervingly to the hope we profess, for he who promised is faithful.
                                    (Hebrews 10:22–23)

Come near to God and he will come near to you.   (James 4:8)

CHAPTER 9

A Love Beyond Comprehension

In this chapter, we are going to talk in a more in-depth way about the love of God. That's easier said than done, though, because God's love is beyond our natural abilities of human comprehension.

The Bible compares the relationship of Jesus Christ and His body, the church, to a marriage relationship: He is our Bridegroom, and we are His bride. If we consider the implications of this analogy, we will come to better understand and appreciate how much God loves us.

Sometimes, we treat God and His Son Jesus Christ in the way that some young women treat their boyfriends and would-be husbands. Take, for example, the young man who is ready to get married and give his girlfriend everything he has. His girlfriend loves him, but she isn't ready to give up the habits of her lifestyle that marriage would require her to sacrifice on his behalf. So, she trusts that he'll wait for her while she "sows her wild oats" and has her fun.

Next, consider a young man who is believing God for a wife. He has a good job and would be able to provide above and beyond the needs of his potential bride. Along comes a woman who takes up with him—not because she loves him, but because he can afford to buy her nice things. He buys her a new car, expensive jewelry, and other "needs," hoping that, one day, she'll love him for who he is and not for what's in his wallet.

These scenarios are exactly what Jesus is getting from His bride—she takes Him for granted and believes she can have her cake and eat it, too; she "loves" Him for what He can give her. But Jesus is saying, "I want My bride to be without spot or wrinkle. (See Ephesians 5:25–27.) I

131

don't want her cheating on Me—flirting with other religions, dabbling in sin, and otherwise tarnishing her character." So many people come to God and say, "God, I need a car. God, I need a raise. I need this, I need that." In reality, they're saying, "I *want* such and such." Now, the Word says that God will supply all of our needs. (See Philippians 4:19.) It also says that He *"will give* [us] *the desires of* [our] *heart,"* but there is a condition: if we *"delight* [ourselves] *in the LORD"* (Psalm 37:4). He is going to give us the desires of our heart, which means He is going to give us more than just our needs. But He is not going to cater to our greed.

> *No matter how tempting we may find certain things of this world, we need to be 100 percent devoted to God and His Son if we expect Jesus to "marry" us.*

When we delight ourselves in the Lord Jesus, we are totally committed to Him; we aren't running around chasing after other "gods." He's not going to be committed to someone who has a lack of fidelity toward Him. That's not what He is looking for in a bride. And neither is God the Father. God is looking for the most incredible bride for His Son—a church without spot or wrinkle. A body of believers who will make a wholehearted commitment to Christ and ignore anything and anyone else who clamors for their attention and allegiance. No matter how tempting we may find certain things of this world, we need to be 100 percent devoted to God and His Son if we expect Jesus to "marry" us.

A MARRIAGE RELATIONSHIP TO THE SON

In marriage, the husband gives himself to his bride, and everything he has becomes hers. The same transaction occurs from the bride's standpoint—all that she is and all that she has becomes his. Now, where our relationship with God is concerned, we give Christ our all because He gave us His all. We definitely get the better end of the deal. And He is waiting for His body—and for you, as an individual—to make that 100 percent commitment. God's love for you is immeasurable—it's beyond comprehension—and He just wants you to love Him in return *"with all your heart and with all your soul and with all your mind and with all your strength"* (Mark 12:30; see also Matthew 22:37; Luke 10:27). There have been times in our lives when we have sinned and not loved God, whether by having a bad attitude, harboring unforgiveness, telling lies, or something else. God is looking for a bride without spot or wrinkle. And what is happening in this day and age is that He is getting ready for this great union between His Son and the bride of Christ by preparing the bride.

Whenever a bride is about to get married, she is traditionally showered with gifts, both at her bridal shower(s) and at the wedding. Similarly, Father God desires to shower us with unimaginable gifts as we prepare for this beautiful time of being the bride of Christ.

In Bible days, it wasn't uncommon for a man and a woman to meet only once before their wedding day. Their union was a type of business arrangement between the bride's father and the groom's father, and it was the father of the groom who decided on the date of the ceremony. The happy couple wouldn't see each other again until the day they were to be married. When the dad told the groom, "Today's the day you're getting married; let's go get her," it was "go" time. That's why it was necessary to be prepared. The bride had to have her wedding dress by her bed, so that no matter what time her groom showed up, she would be ready. And that is how they did it back then. It's a type and shadow of the fact that no matter where we are or what we are doing, we need to be ready for Christ's return. For when the Father tells the Son, "It's time to get Your bride," we must be prepared for Him to come get us. In return, all He asks for is our heart—all of it. He's looking for those who are completely committed to Him.

RENEW YOUR VOWS THROUGH A PRAYER OF REDEDICATION

I want to lead you in a prayer of rededication to God. You might say, "Well, I'm really 'good' with God right now." It still won't hurt you to say this prayer.

Just say, "Father, I have sinned. I don't want to sin anymore. I want to be the bride without a spot, without a wrinkle. I want to be that bride. Take the sin from me. Put it on the cross, never to be held against me again. Father, through the Holy Spirit, lead me and guide me into all that You have for me. Father, show me what it is like to be the bride of

Christ. Father, I thank You for washing me with the water of the Word to take away any spot and any wrinkle or sin before You. I stand before You, pure and holy, in Jesus' name. Thank You, Jesus."

To me, the Jewish custom of the bride needing to be ready for her bridegroom at any time was one of the greatest revelations I have ever seen about how much God is pulling on us to get our act together—to get everything in alignment. Everything that is not of Him needs to be released. It's not worth the cost of eternity. It's just not worth it.

I was praying with a woman who told me, "If my husband were to die right now, he would go to heaven and be embarrassed facing God." It doesn't have to be that way! You have no need to feel embarrassed if you've placed your trust in God and given Him your heart. When you get to heaven, God is going to say, "Well done, thou good and faithful servant. Come on in." (See Matthew 25:21, 23.)

HE'S WAITING FOR YOU

On June 21, 2010, my dad, Charles Hunter, went home to be with the Lord. The day before—June 20—was Father's Day. My dad knew I would come. I had been ministering near Denver, Colorado, and my flight arrived late at night. I went directly to see my dad—I kissed him, hugged him, and told him he was the best dad ever. We got to spend one last Father's Day together. Within twenty-four hours, he was gone.

I'd like to tell you a little more about the relationship I had with my dad. He married my mom, Frances Hunter, and adopted me as his daughter when I was sixteen years old. And, from the first time he met me, he loved me unconditionally—it was a love beyond words, really. He loved me from the moment he found out he was going to be a dad. His enthusiasm could not have been more if my mom had given birth to me again and he was my biological father. And he was the proudest father, which was a great source of encouragement.

If I walked into a room and my dad was there, he would light up like a lightbulb. It was as if there was a floodlight inside of him whose beams glowed outward and lit up the entire room. Even if my husband was with me, Dad would announce, "That's my daughter!" or "That's my girl!" Then, he would greet me and say, "Hi, Joanie baby. I love you."

Shortly after my dad died, I was teaching on unforgiveness. When I came to the part about forgiving your mother and father, I couldn't go on. Mercifully, Kelley came up and finished the teaching for me. The problem was not related to something I needed to forgive but to the fact that I had no recollection of ever having to forgive my dad. He never said a cross word; he never did a mean thing. For weeks, I couldn't make it through that part of the teaching and had to have someone else cover it for me.

> *God is sitting on His throne, and He's waiting for you, too.*

It was special to spend that last Father's Day with my dad. When I went in to greet him, he was lying on his bed in the living room, watching the door, just waiting for his Joanie baby to show up. I could hardly hear him when he spoke, so raspy was his voice, but he mouthed, "Hi, Joanie baby. I love you." And I know how happy he felt to see me, just as he always was, especially when I'd just returned from a trip. He was always lying on his side, watching and waiting for his Joanie baby to walk through the door.

I want to remind you that God is sitting on His throne, and He's waiting for you, too. He is not lying on His side, as my dad was, but He's wondering when you will walk in and spend time with Him. My dad knew that when I walked in, I had carved out time from my busy schedule to visit with him. I would ask his caregiver to leave the room so that we could be together, one-on-one, without anyone else around. Even when my dad could no longer communicate clearly or remember a lot, I remembered a lot about him, and we would just sit there and hold hands, enjoying each other's presence. I would talk to him about what was going on in my life, and then he would try to tell me something. Most of the time, he would just say, "I love you. I'm so proud of you." And he would pat my hand, something he first did the day I met him.

God is waiting for us to carve out time from our busy schedules to come to Him and spend time in His presence. He's sitting there, patiently waiting, knowing that we're busy with work, with children, with household duties, with travel, and so forth. Yet He is so patient. He waits for us to come and spend time with Him, one-on-one, so that we not only know about Him but experience Him and have an intimate relationship with Him.

When my dad died, my experience was completely different from when my mom died. When my dad died, I cried a lot, but not because of trauma; it was grief that caused my tears. I had to really seek God to find out what was causing the tears. It was not heaviness, because I knew that Dad was with Mom in heaven—and, more important, that he was with Jesus. So, I wasn't sad for him. I wasn't sad for me that he was gone, either, and yet I cried and cried and cried. I asked the Father, "God, why am I crying?"

Now, God cleanses us with the washing of the water of the word (see Ephesians 5:26), and that's good. But, sometimes, that cleansing seems to come through our tear ducts. And that is what was happening while I was crying so deeply over my father's death. Again, I wasn't crying tears of sorrow. I knew that my dad had loved me unconditionally—beyond words. I was his world, basically second to Mom. And then, when Mom went, I moved up to number one. On this earth, I was everything to him.

I finally came to realize how much I missed his unconditional love. I missed knowing that he was lying in bed saying, "Oh, Joan's praying for the sick again," or "She's on another airplane, so she won't come to see me." He never griped or complained about my schedule or worried that I wouldn't come to spend time with him. He knew that his Joanie baby would carve out special time to spend with him.

Above everything else, God wants our hearts. He wants our love. He doesn't want our hearts putting anything else above Him. He doesn't want our minds if our hearts are going to other places. It's just like with a husband and wife. For example, a wife may have given her heart to several boyfriends before getting married, and if she hasn't taken back her heart and given it completely and wholly to her husband, problems will arise. It's time for us to free our hearts from entanglement with the things of this world and to give them fully to God, instead.

My prayer is for you to understand the incredible love of God. He loves you so much. Let me reemphasize that as I was praying and asking God why I was crying over the death of my dad, God said, "You miss his unconditional love and the sense of how much he really, really loved you and wanted only the best for you." In His still, small voice, the Holy Spirit whispered to me, "You think he loved you a lot. But that is nothing compared to how much I love you."

Scriptures to Take to Heart

Do not fret because of evil men or be envious of those who do wrong.... Trust in the LORD and do good; dwell in the land and enjoy safe pasture. Delight yourself in the LORD and he will give you the desires of your heart. Commit your way to the LORD; trust in him and he will do this: He will make your righteousness shine like the dawn, the justice of your cause like the noonday sun. Be still before the LORD and wait patiently for him. (Psalm 37:1, 3–7)

The LORD has appeared of old to me, saying: "Yes, I have loved you with an everlasting love; therefore with lovingkindness I have drawn you. Again I will build you, and you shall be rebuilt, O virgin of Israel! You shall again be adorned with your tambourines, and shall go forth in the dances of those who rejoice." (Jeremiah 31:3–4 NKJV)

I pray that you, being rooted and established in love, may have power, together with all the saints, to grasp how wide and long and high and deep is the love of Christ, and to know this love that surpasses knowledge—that you may be filled to the measure of all the fullness of God. (Ephesians 3:17–19)

About the Author

At the tender age of twelve, Joan Hunter committed her life to Christ and began faithfully serving in ministry alongside her parents, Charles and Frances Hunter. Together, they traveled around the globe conducting Healing Explosions and Healing Schools.

Joan is an anointed healing evangelist, a dynamic teacher, and a best-selling author. She is the founder and president of Joan Hunter Ministries, Hearts 4 Him, and 4 Corners Foundation, and she is also the president of Hunter Ministries. Joan's television appearances have been broadcast around the world on World Harvest Network, Inspiration Network, TBN, NRB Word Networks, Daystar, Faith TV, Cornerstone TV, The Church Channel, Total Christian Television, Christian Television Network, Watchmen Broadcasting, and God TV. Joan has also been the featured guest on many national television and radio shows, including Sid Roth's *It's Supernatural!*, *It's a New Day*, *The Miracle Channel*, *The Patricia King Show*, *Today with Marilyn and Sarah*, and many others.

Together, Joan and her powerful international healing ministry have conducted miracle services and healing schools throughout numerous countries in a world characterized by brokenness and pain. Having emerged victorious through tragic circumstances, impossible obstacles, and immeasurable devastation, Joan shares her personal message of hope and restoration to the brokenhearted, deliverance and freedom to the bound, and healing and wholeness to the diseased. Her vision is to see the body of Christ live in freedom, happiness, wholeness, and financial wellness.

Joan lives with her husband, Kelley Murrell, in Pinehurst, Texas. Together, they have eight children—four daughters and four sons— and five grandchildren.